PERFORMANCE PRESENTATION STANDARDS

1993

 Association for Investment Management and Research

Copyright © 1993
Association for Investment Management and Research

Published by

Association for Investment Management and Research
P.O. Box 3668
Charlottesville, Va. 22903
U.S.A.
804/977-6600
Fax 804/977-1103

200 Park Ave., 18th Floor
New York, N.Y. 10166
U.S.A.
212/953-5700
Fax 212/953-5799

AIMR encourages investment and other firms to provide *Standards of Practice Handbook* and *Performance Presentation Standards* to all professional staff members. Additional copies of the *Handbook* are available for purchase at $20 each. A 25 percent discount applies for CFA candidates. Volume discounts are available on orders of 10 or more. Additional copies of *Performance Presentation Standards* are available free of charge to investment practitioners and organizations seeking to educate employees or clients; a fee is charged for other uses. For more information or to place an order, please contact AIMR Publications Sales Department, P.O. Box 7947, Charlottesville, Va. 22906 U.S.A.; 804/980-3647; Fax 804/977-0350.

ISBN: 1-879087-27-8

CONTENTS

Foreword	v
Preface	vii
Summary	ix

Performance Presentation Standards

I.	Preamble		1
II.	Parties Affected		2
III.	Compliance		2
IV.	Performance Calculations		3
	A.	Required Calculations	3
	B.	Recommended Calculations	4
V.	Composites		5
	A.	Construction and Maintenance of Composites	5
	B.	Presentation of Composites	7
	C.	Disclosures	8
VI.	Multiple-Asset Portfolios		9
	A.	Total Return of the Multiple-Asset Composite	9
	B.	Segment Returns as Supplemental Information	9
	C.	Segment Returns as Single-Asset Composites or Added to Single-Asset Composites	10
VII.	Retroactive Compliance		10
	A.	Presentation of Historical Data	10
	B.	Guidelines for Retroactive Compliance	10
VIII.	Measures of Risk and Dispersion		11
	A.	External Risk Measures	11
	B.	Internal Risk Measures	12
IX.	Verification		12
	A.	Level I Verification	12
	B.	Level II Verification	13
X.	Treatment of International Investments		13
	A.	Performance Calculations	13
	B.	Composites	14
	C.	Currency and Currency Overlay Portfolios	15
XI.	Treatment of Real Estate		16
	A.	Performance Calculations	16
	B.	Disclosures	17

XII.	Treatment of Portfolios Using Leverage and/or Derivative Securities		17
	A. Restatement to an All-Cash Basis		17
	B. Disclosure of Strategies		18
	C. Incremental Return Calculation		18

Appendix A
    Performance Calculations 19

Appendix B
    Measures of Risk and Dispersion 33

Appendix C
    International Investments 44

Appendix D
    Examples of Portfolios Using Leverage and/or
      Derivative Securities 52

Appendix E
    SEC Position on Advertising Performance 61

Appendix F
    Portability of Investment Results 63

Appendix G
    Sample Presentations 65

Appendix H
    AIMR Standard of Professional Conduct III F 68

Index 69

FOREWORD

The AIMR Performance Presentation Standards were first introduced, under the auspices of the Financial Analysts Federation, in the September/October 1987 issue of the *Financial Analysts Journal*. The standards were the result of dedicated effort by members of the Committee for Performance Presentation Standards, chaired by Claude N. Rosenberg, Jr., RCM Capital Management. Other committee members included R.H. Jeffrey, Jeffrey Co.; Robert G. Kirby, Capital Guardian Trust Group; Dean LeBaron, CFA, Batterymarch Financial Management; and John J.F. Sherrerd, CFA, Miller, Anderson & Sherrerd. AIMR is grateful to all of these individuals for their important contributions to this long-term project.

Since that time, the standards have been reviewed extensively by members of the industry and revised in response to their many comments and recommendations. The underlying principles, however, have remained the same.

In 1990, after the joining of the Financial Analysts Federation and the Institute of Chartered Financial Analysts into the Association for Investment Management and Research, the AIMR Board of Governors endorsed the standards and approved the establishment of the Performance Presentation Standards Implementation Committee. It was the responsibility of this group to review the standards in light of industry reaction in preparation for the target implementation date of January 1, 1993. Under the inspired leadership of Frederick L. Muller, CFA, Atlanta Capital Management Co., the committee's initial chair, the group began its work. The committee members included Dwight D. Churchill, CFA, CSI Asset Management; Kathleen A. Condon, CFA, Bankers Trust Co.; Thomas S. Drumm, CFA, Keystone Group; the late Creighton E. Gatchell, Jr., CFA, Cunningham, Henderson & Papin (formerly at David L. Babson & Co.); David M. Kirr, CFA, Kirr, Marbach & Co.; Ronald D. Peyton, Callan Associates; Lee N. Price, CFA, RCM Capital Management; R. Charles Tschampion, CFA, General Motors Investment Management Corp.; and Katrina F. Sherrerd, CFA, AIMR, who served as staff liaison. For reasons of continuity, membership in this group has remained unchanged, although leadership of the committee passed to Lee N. Price, CFA, and R. Charles Tschampion, CFA, in 1992, and the staff liaison became Susan Martin, CFA, AIMR. AIMR is indebted to these outstanding professionals, all of whom left their marks on the resultant standards.

This publication incorporates the work of the Implementation Committee and, therefore, the response of AIMR members and other investment professionals who have embraced the idea of establishing a set of guidelines for the presentation of investment performance. The wording of the original standards has been revised—and supplementary material added—as a result of the work of the Implementation Committee and its subcommittees during the past two years.

The development of the standards has not been free of controversy. But this is to be expected in a diverse industry. The standards are the manifestation of a set of guiding ethical principles and should be interpreted as *minimum* standards for presenting investment performance. The standards have been faithfully designed to satisfy several goals: to improve the service offered to investment management clients, to enhance the professionalism of the industry, and to bolster the notion of self-regulation. They have been included as Standard III F of the AIMR Standards of Professional Conduct, effective January 1, 1993. As such, they set expectations for—and provide an industry yardstick for—evaluating fairness and full-disclosure aspects of investment performance presentation.

Several subcommittees have studied issues specific to application of the standards to expanded areas, such as international investing, the treatment of portfolios using leverage and/or derivatives, real estate, and the management of large numbers of small-sized portfolios. Recommendations from these subcommittees are included in this publication. The Implementation Committee was intended to be a standing committee, however, and its work has not ended. AIMR recognizes its responsibility to review the standards on an ongoing basis so that the standards remain current, effectively representing the investment management industry as it evolves.

Darwin M. Bayston, CFA
President and CEO
Association for Investment Management and Research
March 1993

PREFACE

The Performance Presentation Standards Implementation Committee is established as an ongoing AIMR committee with the responsibilities of reviewing the standards as the industry evolves, providing interpretation and clarification, and expanding the principles of the standards as new situations warrant.

The implementation process is designed to be dynamic, allowing for ongoing consideration of implementation issues. As the need arises, the Implementation Committee will establish special subgroups with expertise in specific areas. Areas currently targeted for additional study include venture capital, private placements, broker wrap accounts, and the treatment of after-tax investment results. For these and other situations that have not been directly addressed by the standards, the notion of full disclosure applies. A manager must make good-faith efforts to present sufficiently detailed information so as to present performance accurately.

The committee will also review recommended guidelines as the "state of the art" evolves so that adherence to the standards will provide for a full and fair presentation of investment performance that is in keeping with the highest ethical standards.

We wish to acknowledge the work of the following subcommittees and to thank the members for their contributions:

Leverage/Derivatives Subcommittee: Jeffrey A. Geller, CFA, BEA Associates; William P. Miller, CFA, General Motors Investment Management Corp.; J. Paula Pierce, Commodities Corp. (U.S.A.); R. Charles Tschampion, CFA, General Motors Investment Management Corp.; Jeffrey L. Winter, CFA, QuantiLogic Asset Management Co.

Bank Trust Subcommittee: Kathleen A. Condon, CFA, Bankers Trust Co.; Pamela Havener Conroy, Northern Trust Co.; Richard M. Crouse, Pittsburgh National Bank; Jan A. Koenig, CFA, Texas Commerce Investment Management Co.

International Subcommittee: Phillip Bullen, Baring International Investment Ltd.; Richard Carr, CFA, Brinson Partners, Inc.; Shaw B. Coda-Wagener, CFA, Capital Research International; Karen Prooth, J.P. Morgan; Deborah H. Miller, CFA, Batterymarch Financial Management; Catherine A. Nowinski, Brinson Partners, Inc.; Lee N. Price, CFA, RCM Capital Management; Neil E. Riddles, Templeton International.

Real Estate Subcommittee: Ronald D. Peyton, Callan Associates; Paul S. Saint-Pierre, Lend Lease International Realty Advisors, Inc.; Steven B. McSkimming, Institutional Property Consultants.

In addition, thanks are also extended to the following individuals and organizations, each of whom provided continuing counsel:

Real Estate: Peter Gregovich, Callan Associates; Donald Morse, TCW Realty Advisors; Richard Rosenberg, Callan Associates; Kimberly Smith, Frank Russell Co.; Michael Torres, Wilshire Associates; Christopher Volk, FCA International Advisors; Scott Elliott, Callan Associates; Scott Fong, Callan Associates; Performance Measurement and Reporting Committee of the National Council of Real Estate Investment Fiduciaries; National Association of Real Estate Investment Managers. *Performance Calculations:* Robert Farguharson, Financial Models; Stamos Katotakis, Financial Models; Jeannette R. Kirschman, Russell Private Investments; Ronald D. Peyton, Callan Associates; Kevin Terhaar, CFA, Moreland Management Co. *International:* Arthur W. McCain, InterSec Research Corp.; Chris Nowakowski, InterSec Research Corp.; Ian McAra, Baring International Investment Ltd. *Measures of Risk and Dispersion:* Dwight D. Churchill, CFA, CSI Asset Management; Steven Lee, CSI Asset Management; Gordon Antelman, University of Chicago Graduate School of Business; Barr Rosenberg, Rosenberg Institutional Equity Management; Cecilia Wong, Base-Two Investment Systems, Inc. *Composites:* James E. Hollis III, CFA, Standish, Ayer & Wood, Inc.; Ronald D. Peyton, Callan Associates.

Special thanks are offered to Susan Martin, CFA, who ably served as AIMR staff liaison to the Implementation Committee and whose steady hand guided the preparation of these standards.

Finally, acknowledgement is made of the outstanding contributions of the late Creighton E. Gatchell, Jr., CFA, Cunningham, Henderson & Papin, Inc., who was a member of the Implementation Committee from its inception. The results of Gatchell's hard work and dedication to the committee's goals permeate the standards as well as this publication.

Lee N. Price, CFA
RCM Capital Management
Co-Chair, Performance Presentation Standards Implementation Committee

R. Charles Tschampion, CFA
General Motors Investment Management Corp.
Co-Chair, Performance Presentation Standards Implementation Committee
March 1993

SUMMARY

The Performance Presentation Standards are a set of guiding ethical principles intended to promote full disclosure and fair representation by investment managers in reporting their investment results. A secondary objective is to ensure uniformity in reporting so that results are directly comparable among investment managers. To this end, some aspects of the standards are mandatory (i.e., they *must* be observed); other aspects are recommended (i.e., they *should* be observed). Of course, not every situation can be anticipated, so meeting the full disclosure and fair representation intents also means making a conscientious, good-faith effort to present investment results in a manner consistent with the underlying ethical principles of the standards. This may require going beyond the minimum mandatory requirements and disclosures.

The following is a summary list of (1) the requirements and mandatory disclosures necessary for compliance with the AIMR Performance Presentation Standards and (2) the practices that AIMR recommends. The numbers following each entry refer to the sections of the standards containing full descriptions and explanations.

Requirements

To be considered in compliance, a manager's presentations must incorporate the following practices:

- Use of total return to calculate performance. (IV A 1)
- Use of accrual, as opposed to cash, accounting, except for dividends and calculations of performance for periods prior to 1993. (IV A 2)
- Use of time-weighted rates of return, with valuation on at least a quarterly basis and geometric linking of period returns. (IV A 3)
- Inclusion of cash and cash equivalents in composite returns. (IV A 5)
- Inclusion of all actual, fee-paying, discretionary portfolios in at least one composite. (V A 1)
- No linkage of simulated and model portfolios with actual performance. (V A 2)
- Asset-weighting of composites using beginning-of-period values. (V A 3)
- Addition of new portfolios to a composite after the start of the next performance measurement period or according to reasonable and consistently applied manager guidelines. (V A 6)

- Exclusion of terminated portfolios from a composite for all periods after the last full period they were in place, but inclusion for all periods prior to termination. (V A 7)
- No restatement of composite results following changes in a firm's organization. (V A 9)
- No portability of portfolio results. (V A 9)
- Deduction from gross performance of all trading costs and embedded fees, such as wrap fees, that cannot be unbundled. (IV B 3)
- Presentation of at least a 10-year performance record (or for the period since firm inception, if shorter). (V B 2)
- Presentation of annual returns for all years. (V B 4)

For international portfolios:
- Presentation of subsector, or carve-out, returns as stand-alone composites only as supplemental information unless cash and currency allocation have been separately managed for each subsector. (X B 1)
- Calculation of the benchmark for any currency overlay portfolio in accordance with the mandate of the portfolio, unless the benchmark is actually the currency return on a published benchmark. (X C 2)

For real estate:
- Presentation of returns from income and capital appreciation in addition to total return. (XI A 1)
- Valuation of real estate portfolios at least quarterly. (XI A 2)

Mandatory Disclosures

Performance presentations must disclose the following information:
- The availability of a complete list and description of the firm's composites. (V B 1)
- The number of portfolios and amount of assets in a composite, and the percentage of the firm's total assets the composite represents. (V C 1)
- Whether balanced portfolio segments are included in single-asset composites, and an explanation of how cash has been allocated among asset segments. (V C 2)
- Whether performance results are calculated gross or net of investment management fees; the manager's fee schedule; and for net results, the average weighted management fee. (V C 3)

- The existence of a minimum asset size below which portfolios are excluded from a composite. (V C 4)
- The use of settlement date rather than trade date valuation. (V C 5)
- Whether leverage has been used in portfolios included in a composite, and the extent of its use. (V C 6)
- The inclusion of any non-fee-paying portfolios in composites. (V C 7)
- If performance results are presented after taxes, the tax rate assumption. (IV B 4)

For historical records:
- The full record not being in compliance, if that is the case. (VII A 1)
- The noncompliance periods, if any. (VII A 2)
- A description of how noncompliance periods are out of compliance. (VII A 3)

For international portfolios:
- Whether composites and benchmarks are gross or net of withholding taxes on dividends, interest, and capital gains; if net, the assumed tax rate for the benchmark. (X A 1)
- Whether the composite is a subsector of a larger portfolio, and if so, the percentage of the larger portfolio the subsector represents. (X B 1)
- Whether representative portfolios are used in the returns of subsectors shown as supplemental information. (X B 1)
- For composites managed against specific benchmarks, the percentage of the composites invested in countries or regions not included in the benchmark. (X B 2)
- For returns that exclude the effect of currency, whether the returns are presented in local currency and, if so, a statement that the local currency return does not account for interest rate differentials in forward currency exchange rates. (X C 1)

For real estate:
- The absence of independent appraisals. (XI A 2)
- The source of the valuation, and the valuation policy. (XI A 2)
- The return formula and accounting policies for such items as capital expenditures, tenant improvements, and leasing commissions. (XI B 1)

Recommended Guidelines and Disclosures

AIMR encourages the practices listed below:
- Use of accrual accounting for dividends and for periods prior to 1993. (IV A 2)
- Revaluation of a portfolio whenever cash flows and market action combine to distort performance. (IV B 1)
- Use of trade-date accounting. (IV B 2)
- Presentation of performance gross of investment management fees in one-on-one situations and before taxes (except for international withholding taxes). (IV B 3, IV B 4)
- Consistent treatment of convertible and other hybrid securities across and within composites. (V A 10)
- Provision of the following additional information:
    - External risk measures such as standard deviation of composite returns across time. (VIII A)
    - Benchmarks that parallel the risk or investment style the client portfolio is expected to track. (VIII A 2)
    - Internal risk measures such as dispersion of returns across portfolios in a composite. (VIII B)
    - Cumulative returns for all periods. (V B 4)
    - Portfolio size range for each composite (unless five or fewer portfolios) and the percentage of total assets managed in the same asset class as represented by the composite. (V C 1)
    - If leverage has been used, results on an all-cash (unleveraged) basis, where possible. (XII A)
    - Equal-weighted composites in addition to asset-weighted composites. (V A 5)
    - For composite results that include both taxable and tax-exempt securities, the percentages of each class in the composite and, where possible, returns for each asset class. (V B 5)

For international portfolios:
- Calculation of returns net of withholding taxes on dividends, interest, and capital gains; disclosure of the percentage of the portfolio for which potential capital gains taxes on unrealized gains have not been subtracted. (X A 2)
- Disclosure of inconsistencies among portfolios in the treatment of exchange rates. (X A 4)

- Disclosure of the range or the average country weights of a composite that is managed against a specific benchmark. (X B 2)
- Creation of separate composites for portfolios that allow currency hedging and those that prohibit currency hedging, unless the manager judges the use of hedging to be immaterial, and creation of separate composites for portfolios managed against hedged benchmarks and those that are managed against unhedged benchmarks. (X B 3)
- For a presentation of portfolios excluding the effect of currency, calculation of the return fully hedged back to the base currency of that portfolio. (X C 1)
- Valuation of currency overlay portfolios whenever there are notified changes in the underlying currency exposures (as the result of a shift in the underlying assets). (X C 3)

PERFORMANCE PRESENTATION STANDARDS

I. Preamble

The Association for Investment Management and Research (AIMR) and its subsidiary organizations, the Financial Analysts Federation (FAF) and the Institute of Chartered Financial Analysts (ICFA), formulated these performance presentation standards for investment management results and subsequently endorsed and adopted them. These standards represent the work of the Committee for Performance Presentation Standards, commissioned in 1986 by the FAF; the Performance Presentation Standards Implementation Committee, commissioned by AIMR in 1990; and various subcommittees of the Implementation Committee.

The work toward establishing these standards has been consistently guided by the investment community's need for a common, accepted set of ethical principles ensuring fair representation and full disclosure in investment managers' presentations of their results to clients and prospective clients. A secondary objective is to achieve greater uniformity and comparability among such presentations. Some aspects of the standards are mandatory (i.e., they *must* be observed), and other aspects are recommended (i.e., they *should* be observed). Although the standards specify minimum calculation requirements, they are intended primarily to be performance *presentation* standards, not performance *measurement* standards. It is neither envisioned nor intended that the standards enhance or detract from the potential value or usefulness of the information contained in historical results.

No finite set of guidelines can cover all potential situations or anticipate future developments in industry structure, technology, or practices. Meeting the primary objectives of fair representation and full disclosure requires a conscientious, good-faith commitment to the spirit of the standards under any specific circumstances. Disclosure must be relied upon to convey the elements of any material interpretations that are not covered in the standards. Meeting the full intent of the standards may, and probably will, require more than meeting the minimum requirements and mandatory disclosures. No portion of the standards should be interpreted as inhibiting managers from providing additional information that prospective clients or consultants might request or believe would more clearly represent the manager's investment results.

II. Parties Affected

The standards affect those who present performance information and those who use performance information. All AIMR members, CFAs, and candidates for the CFA designation are required to inform their employers about the existence and content of the standards and to encourage their employers to adopt and use the standards. Such employers include investment advisory firms, banks, insurance companies, consultants and broker–dealer firms acting as investment advisors, as well as other organizations offering investment management services.

For the user audience, the primary application of the standards is in presenting performance to prospective clients. Current clients also must be provided returns that are calculated according to methods that conform to the standards and that are consistent with the calculation methods applied to the manager's composites. Performance presentations in compliance with the standards do not obviate the need for due diligence on the part of prospective clients or consultants in evaluating performance data.

III. Compliance

All portfolios solely invested in U.S. and/or Canadian securities managed for U.S.- or Canada-based clients must be presented in composites that adhere to the AIMR standards to claim compliance as of January 1, 1993, or before. The standards will be implemented for portfolios invested in non-U.S. and/or non-Canadian investments ("international portfolios") as of January 1, 1994. An exemption to the implementation of the standards for taxable portfolios has been granted until January 1, 1994. Firms electing to take advantage of this exemption must disclose in all presentations that they are not in compliance for taxable portfolios. Managers marketing taxable and international portfolios are encouraged to come into compliance during 1993 in preparation for the mandatory January 1, 1994, implementation date.

For periods prior to January 1, 1993, a firm has the option of restating historical performance numbers in accordance with the standards. As long as appropriate disclosures are made, a firm can claim compliance with the standards as of January 1, 1993, and going forward without restating its historical record. The requirements and disclosures for retroactive compliance are presented in Section VII.

The Performance Presentation Standards were incorporated into the AIMR Code of Ethics and Standards of Professional Conduct as of January 1, 1993.

Section III E of the Standards of Professional Conduct prohibits misrepresentation of performance. Section III F specifically endorses the practices set forth in the standards (see Appendix H).

Compliance must be met on a firmwide basis, i.e., selected composites may not be presented as being in compliance unless *all* of the firm's qualifying portfolios have been accounted for in at least one composite. If an autonomous investment firm is itself owned by a larger holding company, or if a subsidiary or division is registered or holds itself out to the public as a separate entity, it may claim full compliance for itself without its parent organization being in compliance. To claim compliance, firms must meet all the requirements and mandatory disclosures and any other additional requirements or disclosures necessary to that firm's specific situation. If results are not in full compliance, performance cannot be presented as being "in compliance except for . . .".

IV. Performance Calculations

Achieving comparability among performance results requires at least some uniformity in methods used to calculate returns. The standards allow flexibility as long as the calculations chosen represent performance fairly and without intent to misrepresent. For additional calculations that apply to international and real estate portfolios, see Sections X and XI. Appendix A provides additional detail on performance calculations.

    A.   *Required Calculations*

        The minimum requirements for calculating returns are as follows:
1. Total return, including realized and unrealized gains and losses plus income, is required.
2. Accrual accounting is required for fixed-income securities and all securities for which income is anticipated, with the exception of dividends. Accrual accounting for dividends as of their ex-dividend date is recommended, but cash-basis accounting is acceptable as long as it does not distort performance. Estimated accrual is acceptable, although exact accrual is preferred. Accrued income must be included in both the beginning and ending portfolio market values or be otherwise accounted for when performance is being calculated. Accrual accounting is recommended but not required when calculating performance prior to January 1993.
3. Time-weighted rate of return is required using a minimum of quarterly valuation and geometric linking of these interim

returns. Approximation methods are acceptable. Because distortions in performance from cash flows will decrease as portfolios are valued more frequently, daily valuations are recommended.
4. The pricing of all assets must be based on a reasonable estimate of current value of assets sold on that date to a willing buyer. In cases of frequently traded securities, standardized pricing quotations must be used and, if necessary, verified. The valuation of real estate assets is described separately in Section XI.
5. Performance results for any portfolio must be presented with cash, cash equivalents, or substitute assets. This applies to single-asset portfolios, multiple-asset portfolios, and the segments of multiple-asset portfolios when used as single-asset composites or when included in single-asset composites. To account for cash or cash equivalents appropriately, cash must be assigned at the beginning of each reporting period after January 1993.
6. The calculation of portfolio return for inclusion in a composite is required to commence either at the beginning of the first full reporting period for which the portfolio is under management or according to reasonable and consistently applied manager guidelines.

B. *Recommended Calculations*

The recommendations for calculating returns are as follows:
1. Revaluation of a portfolio is recommended whenever cash flows and market action combine to cause a material distortion of performance, deemed to be likely when cash flows exceed 10 percent of the portfolio's market value.
2. Trade-date accounting is recommended for calculating performance, although settlement-date accounting is acceptable if disclosed.
3. The calculation of performance prior to the deduction of investment management fees is recommended unless net-of-fee calculations are required to meet Securities and Exchange Commission (SEC) advertising requirements (see Appendix E). When different kinds of fees are embedded in a single fee, as in the case of wrap fees, the manager must deduct from gross performance all fees that cannot be unbundled. Estimated transaction costs are not permitted.

4. The calculation of performance results before taxes is recommended. If results are presented after taxes, the tax rate assumption must be disclosed.

V. Composites

The standards require the use of composites in investment performance presentations. The standards governing composites help ensure that prospective clients have a fair and complete representation of a manager's past performance record. Each composite must comprise portfolios or asset classes representing a similar strategy or investment objective. The construction of multiple composites is required if the use of a single composite would be misleading or otherwise inappropriate in the context of the presentation for which the composite results are being used. For a multiproduct firm, a composite of all of the firm's portfolios is unlikely to be meaningful and is not recommended. A composite could include only one portfolio if the portfolio is unique in its approach but fully discretionary. Mutual funds, commingled funds, or unit trusts may be treated as separate composites or be combined with other portfolios or assets of similar strategies. The performance of portfolios invested in one commingled fund, mutual fund, or unit trust should be represented by the performance of the fund or unit trust. For portfolios invested in more than one fund or unit trust, a total return must also be calculated and performance included in a multiple-asset composite. Balanced portfolios with differing allocations may be defined by allowable bands of asset mix.

    A. *Construction and Maintenance of Composites*
1. All actual, fee-paying, discretionary portfolios must be included in at least one composite. Performance records must be presented fairly and completely without intent to bias or misrepresent by excluding selected portfolios.
2. Firm composites must include only actual assets under management. Model results may be presented as supplementary information, but the model results must be identified as such and must not be linked to actual results.
3. Non-fee-paying portfolios may be included in composites if such inclusion is disclosed.
4. If investment restrictions hinder or prohibit the application of an intended investment strategy, the affected portfolio may be considered nondiscretionary. Examples of such restrictions include:

6 Performance Presentation Standards

    a. Tax considerations that prevent the manager from realizing profits on existing holdings.
    b. Client requirements that the portfolio include or exclude certain securities or types of securities.
    c. Minimum portfolio-size limits that exclude portfolios a manager deems too small to be representative of the manager's intended strategy. The size limit must be disclosed and adhered to rigidly, and no portfolios under the size cutoff can be considered discretionary. Composites of larger sized portfolios must not be used as representative of performance results when marketing to prospective clients whose assets are below the size cutoff.
    d. The definition of a nondiscretionary portfolio depends on a manager's particular strategy. For example, a manager may exclude a South-Africa-free portfolio if that restriction makes its construction different from the manager's other portfolios. Another manager may choose to create a separate composite of several such portfolios. A third manager may include all such portfolios in a more broadly defined composite if the restriction does not result in holdings that are different from the other portfolios' holdings.

5. Asset-weighting of the portfolio returns within a composite is required using beginning-of-period weightings (or beginning-of-period market values plus weighted cash flows, or by aggregating assets and cash flows to calculate performance as for a single portfolio). The additional presentation of equal-weighted composite returns is recommended but not required.

6. New portfolios must not be added to a composite until the start of the next performance measurement period (month or quarter) after the portfolio comes under management or according to reasonable and consistently applied manager guidelines.

7. Portfolios no longer under management must be included in historical composites for the periods they were under management; that is, "survivor" performance results are prohibited. They must be excluded for all periods after the last full period they were in place.

8. Portfolios must not be switched from one composite to another unless documented changes in client guidelines make this

appropriate.
9. Changes in a firm's organization must not lead to an altering of composite results. A change in personnel should be disclosed, but personnel changes must not be used to alter composite performance results. Performance results of a past affiliation must not be used to represent the historical record of a new affiliation or a newly formed entity. Using the performance data from a prior firm as supplemental information is permitted as long as the past record is not linked to the results of the new affiliation. The guiding principle is that performance is the record of the firm, not of the individual. (See Appendix F.)
10. Convertibles or other hybrid instruments should be treated consistently across and within composites, except when meeting client directives. Convertibles should be treated as equity instruments, unless the manager and the client have decided otherwise.

B. *Presentation of Composites*

The presentation of composites is subject to certain mandatory requirements as well as recommended guidelines for providing information that will allow prospective clients to evaluate fairly the representativeness of the composites being presented. (Sample presentations are provided in Appendix G.)

1. Prospective clients must be advised that a list and description of all of a firm's composites is available.
2. At least a 10-year record (or the record since inception of the firm, if shorter) must be presented; presentation of a 20-year record is recommended if the company has been in existence for 20 years.
3. Retroactive compliance is recommended but not required. Section VII details the requirements for presenting performance for periods prior to 1993.
4. For any period for which compliance is claimed, the presentation of annual returns for all years is required to avoid selectivity in time periods presented. Annualized cumulative performance is recommended. Performance for periods of less than one year must not be annualized.
5. When composites include both taxable and tax-exempt securities, the manager should state the percentages of each class

and, where possible, present results for each of the portions separately.
6. Managers should show both internal and external dispersion of portfolio returns in the composite. Section VIII details the recommendations for the presentation of measures of risk and dispersion.
7. Presentation of supplemental information is recommended when the manager deems this additional information to be valuable to clients. Such disclosures might include the average market capitalization of stocks held, the average quality and duration of bond holdings, and additional information on international portfolios (Section X), real estate portfolios (Section XI), and portfolios using leverage or derivative securities (Section XII). This information must not supplant the required information, and it must be accompanied by the appropriate composite returns.

C. *Disclosures*

The following disclosures are required for each period for which composite results are presented. Additional disclosures will probably be needed to meet the fair-representation and full-disclosure objectives. The disclosures are expected to be specific to each circumstance and are therefore not required in all situations. For additional disclosures that apply to international and real estate portfolios, see Sections X and XI.

1. For each time period for which composite results are presented, a manager must disclose the number of portfolios in the composite, total composite assets, and composite assets as a percentage of firm assets. For composites of five or fewer portfolios, the disclosure "five or fewer portfolios" may be made rather than disclosing the exact number of portfolios. Additional disclosures, such as portfolio size range and the percentage of total assets managed in the same asset class as represented by the composite, are recommended.
2. Disclosure is required of whether segments of multiple-asset, or balanced, portfolios are included in single-asset composites. If they are, a description must be provided of how cash has been allocated to the included asset segments.
3. Disclosure is required of whether performance results are calculated gross or net of investment management fees. In either case, an appropriate schedule of fees must be presented.

When net-of-fee results are presented, the weighted average fee must also be presented so that performance can be computed on a gross-of-fee basis.
4. The existence of a minimum asset size below which portfolios are excluded from a composite must be disclosed.
5. The use of settlement-date rather than trade-date accounting must be disclosed.
6. The use and extent of leverage must be disclosed. (See Section XII and Appendix D.)
7. The inclusion of any non-fee-paying portfolios in composites must be disclosed.
8. If a manager claims current compliance with the standards, but the pre-1993 historical record is not in compliance for all periods, the manager must follow the rules and guidelines in Section VII, Retroactive Compliance.

VI. Multiple-Asset Portfolios

Multiple-asset portfolios are any portfolios that include more than one asset class. Total return on the entire portfolio is required for purposes of composites whenever the manager has discretion over changes from one asset class to another. If the segments of multiple-asset portfolios are broken out separately as supplemental information to the total return or as stand-alone composites of single-asset strategies or if the segments are added to single-asset composites, the manager must meet certain specific requirements to claim compliance with the standards. The standards do not require these subcomponents to be broken out or included in single-asset composites, although managers may choose to do so.

A. *Total Return of the Multiple-Asset Composite*
When a manager uses the total return of a multiple-asset composite to market a multiple-asset portfolio strategy, cash allocation to each of the segments of the multiple-asset composite is not required.

B. *Segment Returns as Supplemental Information*
When a manager uses the total return of a multiple-asset composite to market a multiple-asset portfolio strategy, but the manager wishes to present the segment returns of the multiple-asset composite as supplemental information, the segment returns may be shown without making a cash allocation as long as the returns for each of the composite's segments (including the cash segment)

10 Performance Presentation Standards

are shown along with the composite's total return (see sample presentation in Appendix G).

C. *Segment Returns as Single-Asset Composites or Added to Single-Asset Composites*

When the segment returns of a multiple-asset composite are added to, or are being used to market, single-asset strategies, a cash allocation to each of the segments must be made at the beginning of each reporting period, and the methodology must be disclosed. The segment may then be included on the firm's list of composites. Asset-only returns must not be mixed with asset-plus-cash returns. Section VII details the requirements for retroactive compliance.

VII. Retroactive Compliance

The requirements and disclosures for retroactive compliance apply to any composites constructed for periods prior to January 1993. After this date, all composites must be constructed and maintained in accordance with the standards. For periods prior to January 1993, a firm has the option of restating historical performance numbers in accordance with the standards. As long as appropriate disclosures are made, a firm can claim compliance with the standards as of January 1993 and going forward without restating its historical record. Presentation of a minimum of a 10-year performance record (or since firm inception, if shorter) is required even if the record is not restated.

A. *Presentation of Historical Data*

If a manager claims current compliance with the standards, but the pre-1993 historical record is not in compliance for all periods and the noncompliance periods are linked to periods that are in compliance, the manager must:
1. Disclose that the full record is not in compliance.
2. Identify the noncompliance periods.
3. Explain how the noncompliance periods are out of compliance.

B. *Guidelines for Retroactive Compliance*

The standards for retroactive compliance for periods prior to January 1993 are somewhat more relaxed than the standards that apply after that date.
1. Valuation periods may be as long as one year, although if cash flows were significant during the year, valuations should be done more frequently to reduce performance distortion. To

qualify for inclusion in a composite that is valued annually, a portfolio must have been under management according to a strategy appropriate to the composite for at least one year.
2. Composites may be asset weighted using annual beginning-of-period market values.
3. Accrual accounting need not be applied if cash-basis accounting was used historically.
4. Within multiple-asset portfolios, if cash allocations are made to each of the composite segments, the manager must use a reasonable and consistent approach, and the manager must disclose the methodology used for assigning cash. If information is not available for making a reasonable allocation, then retroactive allocations of each must not be attempted.

VIII. Measures of Risk and Dispersion

The standards recommend presentation of risk measures appropriate to the strategy represented by a composite. Both external and internal risk measures should be considered in presenting performance results. (Appendix B presents examples of how to calculate measures of risk and dispersion.)

A. *External Risk Measures*

External risk measures represent the riskiness of investment strategies and include standard deviation across time, beta, duration, and others that are based on current and historical data. Benchmarks, including market indexes, manager universes, and normal portfolios, provide a relative measure for the riskiness of a strategy.

1. Managers should designate a benchmark and explain this choice.
2. Benchmarks must be consistently applied and must parallel the risk or investment style the client portfolio is expected to track. A portfolio with, for example, 50 percent of its total assets in small- to medium-capitalization stocks and 50 percent in large-capitalization stocks should be compared to a similarly weighted composite of appropriate indexes rather than to just one index. Disclosure of differences in portfolio structure relative to the benchmark is recommended.
3. If an index is used as a benchmark, it should be investable, although this may be impossible with certain indexes such as

some fixed-income and international indexes.
4. For multiple-asset portfolios, managers and clients should agree in advance on the frequency and the assumptions to be used in rebalancing to the benchmark or target allocation.

B. *Internal Risk Measures*

Internal risk measures represent the consistency of a manager's results with respect to the individual portfolio returns within a composite. For an equal-weighted composite, standard deviation across portfolios is the appropriate measure of internal risk. For an asset-weighted composite, a reformulation of the standard deviation to an asset-weighted dispersion measure or an alternative approach to exhibit consistency is recommended. Also recommended is inclusion of the range of portfolio returns within the composite, high–low portfolio return statistics, and other measures a manager deems valuable.

IX. Verification

The standards recommend verification of claims that performance is in compliance. Verification must be performed by an independent party. Two levels of verification are possible. Level I verification applies to the firm; Level II verification includes Level I verification and applies to specific composites.

As in an audit, a relatively small sample of data may satisfy the verifier that appropriate procedures and computer software are in place to calculate performance correctly if no discrepancies are found. The lack of explicit audit trails or apparent errors, however, may warrant a larger sample or additional verification procedures. The verifier may conclude that, based on insufficient backup, some performance records simply do not lend themselves to an attest. A qualified opinion must be issued in such cases, clarifying why a completely satisfactory opinion was not possible. Appendix G provides sample verification statements.

A. *Level I Verification*

A Level I verification attests to the fact that all of a firm's actual, discretionary, fee-paying portfolios are included in at least one composite. Examination procedures generally include verification of the following:
1. Each portfolio, including those no longer under management, is in fact either included in a composite or has been docu-

mented as being excluded for valid reasons.
2. All portfolios sharing the same guidelines are included in the same composite and shifts from one composite to another are based on documented client guidelines.
3. Portfolio returns within the composites are weighted by size.
4. Performance is being calculated using a time-weighted rate of return, with a minimum of quarterly valuations and accrual of income.
5. Disclosures offered to ensure that performance has been presented accurately and in keeping with a full and fair presentation of investment results.

B. *Level II Verification*
A Level II verification examines both the investment management process (tests of validity and propriety of underlying shares, income, and pricing data) and the measurement of performance (computation and presentation of performance data). Examination procedures generally include verification of the following:
1. All of a firm's actual, discretionary, fee-paying portfolios are included in at least one composite (i.e., a Level I verification).
2. Performance calculations use the time-weighted return formula.
3. Asset prices.
4. Capital gains/losses.
5. Trades, on a sample basis, checking the accounting trail, cost records, and actual shares or bonds still held.
6. Income streams, on a sample basis, including the timing and actual receipt of dividends, accrued interest, and the treatment of fees.
7. Cash flows are accounted for properly.

X. Treatment of International Investments

For managers marketing international products, the following additional requirements, disclosures, and recommendations apply. (Appendix C provides additional discussion of issues pertaining to international investments).

A. *Performance Calculations*
In addition to the requirements in Section IV, Performance Calculations, the following requirements and recommendations apply specifically to international portfolios:

1. Managers must disclose whether composite and benchmark returns are net or gross of foreign withholding taxes on dividends, interest, and capital gains. If net performance is shown, managers must also disclose the assumed tax rate for the benchmark.
2. Managers should calculate portfolio returns net of withholding taxes on dividends, interest, and capital gains, and disclose the percentage of the portfolio for which potential capital gains taxes on unrealized gains have not been subtracted. This particularly applies to emerging market investments.
3. Because of the volatility and lengthy settlement periods of some markets, trade-date rather than settlement-date reporting is strongly recommended.
4. A consistent source of period-end exchange rates should be used. Managers should disclose any inconsistencies among portfolios in the treatment of exchange rates.

B. *Composites*

In addition to the requirements in Section V, Composites, the following requirements and disclosures apply specifically to international composites:

1. Subsectors, or carve-outs, of larger international portfolios may be used to create stand-alone composites only if the subsectors are actually managed as separate entities with their own cash allocations and currency management. Disclosure that the composite is a subsector is required. If a stand-alone composite is formed using subsectors from multiple composites, its return must be presented with a list of the underlying composites from which the subsector was drawn, along with the percentage of each composite the subsector represents.

    If the subsector is not treated as a separate entity, the subsector-only performance must be provided as supplemental information to the composite or composites from which the subsector was drawn. In this case, the percentage of the composite's assets represented by the subsector must be disclosed; returns of the larger composite must be made available. Subsector results should include all qualifying portfolios; the presentation of subsector results as supplemental information, however, may be based on representative portfolios as long as this is disclosed. Carve-outs presented as supplemental information must not be combined with stand-alone portfolios.
2. For portfolios managed to a specific international benchmark,

the manager must disclose the percentage of composite assets invested in countries or regions outside the benchmark. The manager should also disclose the range or average of country weights in the composite.
   3. If a composite is to be compared to an unhedged benchmark, portfolios that are allowed to use currency hedging should not be included with portfolios that cannot use hedging instruments, unless the use of currency hedging is judged to be immaterial. Similarly, if portfolios managed against hedged benchmarks are materially different from portfolios managed against unhedged benchmarks, they should be placed in separate composites.
C. *Currency and Currency Overlay Portfolios*
   The requirements below, except for C.1, apply to portfolios managed as stand-alone currency overlay portfolios. (Appendix C provides a description of currency overlays.)
   1. When expressing the return of a portfolio excluding the effect of currency, the return should be shown fully hedged back to the base currency of that portfolio. If this hedged return is not calculated, disclosure must be made that the return is in the local currency and does not account for interest rate differentials in forward currency exchange rates.
   2. The benchmark for any currency overlay portfolio must be calculated in accordance with the mandates of the portfolio (unless the benchmark is actually the currency return on a published benchmark).
   3. Currency overlay portfolios should be valued whenever there are notified changes in the underlying currency exposures (as the result of a shift in the underlying assets). In accordance with the overall standards, currency overlay portfolios must be valued at least quarterly; however, the volatile nature of these portfolios may make the use of shorter time periods necessary to obtain full and fair disclosure.
   4. In terms of currency exposure, composites must be determined according to similar benchmarks and restrictions. In currency management, the underlying currency exposure might not matter if portfolios are managed according to similar index benchmarks. If, however, the manager is being measured according to the value added over existing positions, then the underlying

currency exposure becomes critical. In this case, grouping currency overlay portfolios into composites of more than one portfolio would not be meaningful. A series of one-portfolio composites may be used if composites of multiple currency overlay portfolios would not provide useful information.

XI. Treatment of Real Estate

Because of its unique characteristics, particularly the lack of a readily verifiable secondary market to determine asset values, real estate performance presentation guidelines warrant separate treatment. Consistent with the requirements presented in Section V, Composites, all properties must be included in at least one composite and a list of the composites must be made available. Because of the unique nature of individual real estate investments, however, composites containing single properties will be appropriate in many cases. Presentations should disclose inclusions and exclusions. (Appendix G provides a sample real estate presentation.)

    A.   *Performance Calculations*

        In addition to the requirements in Section IV, Performance Calculations, the following requirements and recommendations apply specifically to real estate portfolios:

        1.   The attribution and separate presentation of returns from income and capital appreciation is required. When presenting the components of total return, the recognition of income at the investor level is preferred over income at the operating level. Appreciation includes realized and unrealized gains and losses.

        2.   The value of a real estate portfolio must be reviewed at least quarterly. Valuations must be performed by independent, objective appraisers with sufficient frequency, not longer than every three years, and the frequency of the valuation must be disclosed. The appraisers must be asked to originate and communicate value rather than merely confirm prior knowledge. The source of the valuation and the valuation policy must be fully disclosed. If client agreements do not require independent appraisals, independent valuations are not required, but the absence of independent valuations must be disclosed.

3. Investment income must be calculated on an accrual basis rather than on a cash basis.
4. Returns associated with cash, cash equivalents, and substitute assets held in the portfolio must be included in the presentation.

B. *Disclosures*

In addition to the required disclosures outlined in previous sections, the following disclosures must be made in the presentation of real estate performance:

1. Return formulas and accounting policies for items such as capital expenditures, tenant improvements, and leasing commissions. A statement as to whether the returns have been audited must be included.
2. The amount of leverage used, if any.
3. The management fee structure, including its relationship to asset valuation.

XII. Treatment of Portfolios Using Leverage and/or Derivative Securities

The standards require that the use and extent of leverage be disclosed when reporting performance. Examples of leverage include, but are not limited to, buying securities on margin, writing covered call options, buying protective put options, using futures for either hedging or speculation, and short-selling. The important issue relating to leverage is the altered risk and return profile of the portfolio. Disclosure of portfolio strategies included in the composite is required when such strategies have significant potential to influence the risk and/or return characteristics of the composite. (Appendix D sets forth examples of the use of leverage and/or derivative securities and provides a discussion of the recommended treatment for performance presentation.)

A. *Restatement to an All-Cash Basis*

Return results should be restated to an all-cash basis when the portfolio used leverage and the same securities could have been purchased at the same prices if the portfolio had the cash to do so. Results should be restated to an all-cash basis only when the necessary restatement can be based entirely on actual transactions and can be verified in accordance with applicable accounting standards, including third-party documentation (such as client agreements about asset allocation or client guidelines on portfolio strategies and objectives).

B. *Disclosure of Strategies*

The standards recommend complete disclosure regarding the nature of the strategies for portfolios using derivative securities. The disclosures must include:
1. A description of the use of derivatives.
2. The amounts of derivatives used.
3. The frequency of their use.
4. A discussion of their characteristics.

These disclosures must be detailed enough for clients or prospective clients to judge the impact of all the pertinent factors regarding the returns and risks of the strategy or portfolio.

C. *Incremental Return Calculation*

The incremental return from derivative securities is equal to the difference between the total fund return and the return on the fund without the contribution of the derivative securities. The incremental return should be calculated whenever (1) such a calculation is representative of the true incremental return attributable to derivatives, and (2) the necessary calculation is based entirely on actual transactions or on third-party documentation that can verify the calculation. Causes of nonrepresentative calculations include, but are not limited to, the use of derivatives affecting the execution of the portfolio strategy in the remainder of the fund or affecting prices of transactions in the remainder of the fund.

APPENDIX A
PERFORMANCE CALCULATIONS

This appendix details performance calculations for portfolios and composites. The intent is not to require revision of existing performance calculations or associated computer software that conform to the concepts of quarterly, time-weighted total returns. Rather, for those who desire a single guideline, widely used definitions, formulas, and methodologies are included for each area of consideration.

Reporting the Performance of Portfolios

The performance of portfolios must be reported using the time-weighted rate of return, as well as total return. The calculation of total return where there are no cash flows for a period (i.e., a month or quarter) is generally straightforward. The formula for calculating total return is:

$$R_{TR} = \frac{MVE - MVB}{MVB}$$

where R_{TR} is the total return (sometimes referred to as the "nonweighted rate of return");
MVE is the market value of the portfolio at the end of the period, including all income accrued up to the end of the period; and
MVB is its market value at the beginning of the period, including all income accrued up to the end of the previous period.

This well-known formula represents growth (or decline) in the value of a portfolio, including both capital appreciation and income, as a proportion of the starting market value. This unweighted rate of return represents a reasonable way of presenting the performance of a portfolio over a period with no cash flows out of, or into, the portfolio. This condition, however, is frequently violated in the normal management of a client's account. Cash flows *do* occur, often unpredictably.

If cash flows occur during the period, they must theoretically be used, in effect, to "buy" additional units of the portfolio at the market price on the day they are received. Thus, the most accurate approach is to calculate the market value of the portfolio on the date of each cash flow, calculate an interim rate

Association for Investment Management and Research

20 Appendix A

of return for the subperiod according to the above formula, and then link the subperiod returns to get the return for the month or quarter. This approach removes the effect of each cash flow. Methods that use this approach, or an approximation of it, are called time-weighted rate of return methods.

Time-Weighted Rate of Return

This section describes three methods to compute time-weighted rate of return. The first is the daily valuation method (or valuation whenever cash flows occur), which is preferred. Two other methods result in approximations of the daily valuation method. They are the modified Dietz method and the modified Bank Administration Institute (BAI) method.

Daily Valuation Method. The formula for valuing the portfolio whenever cash flows occur is:

$$R_{DAILY} = (S_1 \times S_2 \times \ldots S_n) - 1$$

where S_1, S_2, through S_n are the subperiod indexes for subperiods 1, 2, through n.

Note that calculating R_{DAILY} does not require determining the subperiod returns. If desired, the subperiod return, R_i, can be determined from the subperiod index by the formula:

$$R_i = S_i - 1$$

There will always be one more subperiod than there are cash flows in the period. Subperiod 1 extends from the first day of the period up to and including the date of the first cash flow. Subperiod 2 begins the next day and extends to the date of the second cash flow, and so forth. The final subperiod extends from the day after the final cash flow through the last day of the period.

Each of the subperiod indexes is calculated using the formula:

$$S_i = \frac{MVE_i}{MVB_i}$$

where MVE_i is the market value of the portfolio at the end of subperiod i, before any cash flows in period i but including accrued income for

Association for Investment Management and Research

the period, and

MVB_i is the market value at the end of the previous subperiod (i.e., the beginning of this subperiod), including any cash flows at the end of the previous subperiod and including accrued income.

The chief advantage of this method is that it calculates the true time-weighted rate of return, rather than an estimate. The major drawback is that it requires precise valuation of the portfolio on the date of each cash flow, something that is not always feasible or practical. Also, if all securities are not accurately priced for each subperiod valuation, errors generated in the return calculation using the daily valuation method may be greater than the errors caused by using the approximation methods.

Modified Dietz Method. The Dietz method overcomes the need to know the valuation of the portfolio on the date of each cash flow by assuming a constant rate of return on the portfolio during the period. The original Dietz method assumed that all cash flows occurred at the mid-point of the period. The modified Dietz method weights each cash flow by the amount of time it is held in the portfolio. The formula for estimating the time-weighted rate of return using the modified Dietz method, R_{DIETZ}, is:

$$R_{DIETZ} = \frac{MVE - MVB - F}{MVB + FW}$$

where MVB is the market value at the beginning of the period, including accrued income from the previous period;
MVE is the market value at the end of the period, including accrued income for the period;
F is the sum of the cash flows within the period (contributions to the portfolio are positive flows, and withdrawals or distributions are negative flows); and
FW is the sum of each cash flow, F_i, multiplied by its weight, W_i.

W_i is the proportion of the total number of days in the period that the cash flow F_i has been in (or out of) the portfolio. The formula for W_i is:

$$W_i = \frac{CD - D_i}{CD}$$

22 Appendix A

where CD is the total number of days in the period, and
D_i is the number of days since the beginning of the period in which cash flow F_i occurred.

The numerator is based on the assumption that the cash flows occur at the end of the day. If cash flows are assumed to occur at the beginning of the day, the numerator would be $CD + 1 - D_i$. It is important to be consistent, whichever method is chosen.

The chief advantage of the modified Dietz method is that portfolio valuation is not required for the date of each cash flow. Its chief disadvantage is that it provides a less accurate estimate of the true time-weighted rate of return. Specifically, the estimate suffers most when a combination of the following conditions exists: (1) One or more large cash flows occur, and (2) cash flows occur during periods of high market volatility, i.e., the portfolio's returns have been significantly nonlinear.

Modified BAI Method. The modified BAI method determines the internal rate of return (IRR) for the period. Like the original Dietz method, the original BAI method was modified to take into effect the exact timing of each cash flow.

The IRR is that value of R that satisfies the following equation:

$$MVE = \sum F_i (1 + R)^{W_i}$$

where MVE and W_i are the same as for the modified Dietz method. The cash flows, F_i, are also the same as with the Dietz method, with one important exception: The market value at the start of the period is also treated as a cash flow, i.e, $MVB = F_0$.

IRR is obtained by selecting values for R and solving the equation until the result equals MVE. For example, if there are three cash flows (including the market value at the start of the period), there will be three terms in the computational formula:

$$MV_{END} = F_0(1 + R)^{W_0} + F_1(1 + R)^{W_1} + F_2(1 + R)^{W_2}.$$

The first term deals with the first cash flow, F_0, which is the value of the portfolio at the beginning of the period. W_i is the proportion of the period that the cash flow F_i was in (or out) of the portfolio. Because F_0 is in for the whole period, $W_0 = 1$. The larger the value of F_i in the term, the more it will contribute

Association for Investment Management and Research

to the total. But the smaller the exponent (i.e., the value of W_i), the less the term will contribute to the sum. This usually means that the first term, with a large F_0 and $W_0 = 1$, will contribute far more than the other terms.

The advantages and disadvantages of the modified BAI method are the same as those of the modified Dietz method. The modified BAI method has the additional disadvantage of requiring an iterative solution process. This makes BAI less desirable than Dietz when manual calculation is required. However, calculator and computer programs are available for solving IRR.

It should be noted that the modified Dietz method is identical to the first-order approximation of the modified BAI method. For most purposes, the second-order approximation provides sufficiently accurate results.

Performance Gross or Net of Fees

The Performance Presentation Standards mandate that any presentation of performance results indicate whether the portfolio results were computed before investment management fees (i.e., gross of fees) or after (i.e., net of fees). The standards recommend that performance be presented gross of management fees, except where this will conflict with the SEC's position on advertising performance. The choice of net versus gross is left to the manager, as long as the manager discloses which method is being used and includes a fee schedule. When net-of-management-fee composite results are shown, the manager must also disclose the weighted average fee.

AIMR prefers that performance results be presented gross (before deduction) of management fees. This is because a manager's fee schedule is usually scaled to size of assets. Therefore, performance results after deduction of an average management fee will not be representative of results for a portfolio that is much larger or much smaller than the size of the portfolio represented by the average fee. AIMR feels it is more representative to show results before the deduction of management fees and to provide a fee schedule that represents the fee that would actually be paid by the prospective client.

In addition, because fees are sometimes negotiable, presenting performance gross of fees shows the manager's expertise in managing assets without the impact of negotiating skills on the part of the manager or the manager's clients.

Differences in performance results occur when portfolio performance is reported gross of management fees versus net of management fees. Examples using three periods—1, 2, and 10 years—will illustrate what happens when total return is computed gross of fees and net of fees.

Assume a portfolio that has a steady investment return, gross of fees, of 0.5

24 Appendix A

percent per month and total management fees of 0.05 percent per month of the market value of the portfolio on the last day of the month. Management fees are deducted from the market value of the portfolio on that day. There are no cash flows during the period.

In this simple situation, the value of the portfolio gross of fees at the end of any month i (GMV_i) is given by the following formula:

$$GMV_i = MV_{START}\,(1 + R_{GOF})^i$$

where MV_{START} is the market value of the portfolio at the start of the period, and

             R_{GOF} is the monthly investment return, gross of fees.

The value of the portfolio net of management fees for any month i (NMV_i) is its value after such fees are deducted. This quantity is given by:

$$NMV_i = NMV_{i-1}(1 + R_{GOF})(1 - F)$$

where NMV_{i-1} is the market value, less management fees, of the portfolio at the end of the previous month, and

             F is the fee rate, expressed as a proportion.

Because fees are tied to the market value of the portfolio, this equation simply states that the value (net of fees) for the portfolio is last month's net-of-fees value times this month's growth. This result is multiplied by a factor $(1 - F)$ that reduces it by the amount of this month's management fees.

For the first month of the period then, the net-of-fees market value, NMV_1, is:

$$NMV_1 = MV_{START}(1 + R_{GOF})(1 - F)$$

The value for the second month of the period, NMV_2, is:

$$\begin{aligned}NMV_2 &= NMV_1(1 + R_{GOF})(1 - F) \\ &= [MV_{START}(1 + R_{GOF})(1 - F)](1 + R_{GOF})(1 - F) \\ &= MV_{START}(1 + R_{GOF})^2(1 - F)^2\end{aligned}$$

The general formula for computing the market value of our example portfolio, net of fees, for any month i, is:

Association for Investment Management and Research

$$NMV_i = MV_{START}(1 + R_{GOF})^i(1 - F)^i$$

Given these formulas, it is a simple matter to calculate the total return, gross versus net of fees, for any period. Total return for the period ending with month i, assuming no cash flows, is:

$$R_{TOTAL} = \frac{MV_i - MV_{START}}{MV_{START}}$$

where MV_i is GMV_i or NMV_i, depending on whether the calculation is of total return gross or net of fees.

In the example, the return before fees, R_{GOF}, is 0.5 percent (0.005). Fee rate, F, is 0.05 percent (0.0005). Using these values, the total returns, gross and net of fees, for 1, 2, and 10 years (i.e., 12, 24, and 120 months) are shown in Table A-1.

Table A-1. Gross-of-Fees versus Net-of-Fees Example

Period	Total Return Gross of Fees	Total Return Net of Fees	Basis Points Differential
1 year	6.17%	5.54%	63
2 years	12.72	11.38	134
10 years	81.94	71.39	1,055

The table shows that the total return during the first two years is 134 basis points lower when performance is presented net of fees. By the end of the tenth year, this difference has grown to more than 1,000 basis points. Of course, the magnitude of the difference between gross-of-fee and net-of-fee returns will depend on a variety of factors, and the example is purposely simplified. But it illustrates the marked difference in total return that the two ways of presenting results can yield. It also shows that, assuming that other factors such as investment return and fees remain constant, the difference increases due to the compounding effect over time.

Net-of-Fee Calculation. In a net-of-fee calculation, when fees are paid from the corpus of the fund, the payments should be included as a withdrawal of capital in F (flows) and in FW (weighted flows). In addition, performance results are reduced by deducting fees as negative income in the numerator. Using the modified Dietz method to illustrate, the net-of-fee return is

$$R = \frac{MVE - MVB - F - Fees}{MVB + FW}$$

In this example, *MVE* (which includes accrued income for the period) is reduced by the fees. Because fees have been paid out of the account, they should be treated the same as any other negative flow or withdrawal. In other words, *F* includes the (negative) fee payment. The fees now need to be deducted from the numerator to reduce the gross return to a net return.

When the fee is paid by an external source, it must be subtracted from only the numerator because it has not reduced *MVE* nor been included in the calculation of *F*. The formula, however, is the same. This calculation has the same impact of reducing investment earnings by the amount of the fee without any cash flow adjustment.

Cash versus Accrual. The AIMR Performance Presentation Standards mandate that, with the exception of dividends and retroactive performance reporting, interest income be calculated on an accrual basis. The standards recommend that dividends and retroactive performance also be calculated on an accrual basis.

The guiding principle to use in determining what income to report is as follows: Include the income if that income would have been received had the security actually been sold at the end of the performance period. For example, dividends are not payable unless the stock was owned on the ex-dividend date. Therefore, dividends should be accrued as income on the ex-dividend date for trade date valuations. This is not mandatory. On the other hand, most fixed-income securities accrue income on a *pro-rata* basis. This income is payable at the coupon date or when the security is sold.

Interest should be accrued for a security in the portfolio using whatever method is customary and appropriate for that security. The most frequently used way of accruing interest on a U.S. fixed-income security, other than U.S. Treasury issues, is the 30/360-day count method. This method assumes that each month has 30 days, and it assumes a 360-day year. The formula for calculating the number of days over which interest has accrued, using the 30/360-day count method, is:

$$360(Y_2 - Y_1) + 30(M_2 - M_1) + (D_2 - D_1)$$

where Y_1 is the year;
M_1 is the month;
D_1 is the day of the previous coupon date; and

Y_2, M_2, and D_2 are the year, month, and day of the settlement date.

In calculating accrued interest over a performance period, Y_2, M_2, and D_2 can refer to the end-of-period date and Y_1, M_1, and D_1 to the end-of-period date of the previous period.

Some U.S. Treasury discount instruments and zero-coupon bonds already include accrued income as part of their market prices. If income for these instruments is being accrued as part of the income process, it should be deducted from the market price to avoid counting this accrued income twice. That is, market price should be divided into two amounts—the principal amount and the accrued interest.

Reporting the Performance of Composites

A composite is made up of a set of individual portfolios or asset classes. The composite return is intended to be a single value that reflects the overall performance (the "central tendency") of the set. The objective in reporting the returns of composites is to use a method for reporting the composite return that will give the same value achieved if the composite were treated as one master portfolio. That is, the value being calculated is the same value that would result if all of the assets and transactions of the individual portfolios/classes were combined and the return were computed using the procedures discussed earlier.

Four methods might be used to obtain a composite return:

■ *The equal-weighted return (simple average).* The equal-weighted return will only meet the objective in the unlikely event that the market values of all portfolios are exactly the same or all portfolio returns are identical. On the other hand, the simple average, together with the standard deviation, provides measures of the ability of a manager to obtain consistent returns for all portfolios, regardless of size.

■ *The asset-weighted return (market-value-weighted average).* It seems reasonable that, if a composite contains two portfolios, one of which is 10 times the size of the other, the rate of return for the larger portfolio should have more impact on the composite return than the smaller portfolio. The asset-weighted return does this by weighting the contributions to the composite rate of return by the beginning market values of its constituent portfolios. This method will give the same value as if the composite were treated as one master portfolio.

■ *The asset-weighted and cash-flow-weighted return method.* Consider the case in which one of two portfolios in a composite doubles in market value as the result of a contribution on the first day of a performance period. Under the asset-weighted approach, this portfolio will be weighted in the composite based solely on its beginning market value (i.e., not including the contribution). The asset-weighted and cash-flow-weighted approach resolves this problem by including the effect of cash flows in the weighting calculation, as well as in the market values.

■ *The aggregate method.* This method combines the composite assets and cash flows to calculate performance as if the composite were one portfolio. This method is also acceptable as an asset-weighted approach.

The AIMR Performance Presentation Standards mandate that the returns of composites be asset-weighted, although equal-weighted returns can be reported in addition. The asset-weighted and cash-flow-weighted method represents a refinement to the asset-weighted approach. It may be used in place of the straight asset-weighted method.

The equal-weighted return is the simple (unweighted) mean of the individual portfolio returns. The formula for the equal-weighted composite return, C_{EQUAL}, is:

$$C_{EQUAL} = \frac{R_1 + R_2 + \ldots R_n}{n}$$

where R_1 is the return for the first portfolio in the composite, and
           n is the number of portfolios in the composite.

The asset-weighted composite return, C_{ASSET}, may be calculated using the formula:

$$C_{ASSET} = \frac{\Sigma P_i}{MVB_{TOTAL}}$$

where ΣP_i is the sum of the weighted returns for the portfolios within the composite, and
           MVB_{TOTAL} is the total market value at the beginning of the period for all the portfolios within the composite. (Note that any portfolios added or terminated during the period should not be included in this calculation.)

Each of these weighted portfolio returns is calculated using the formula:

$$P_i = MVB_i \times R_i$$

where   MVB$_i$ is the beginning market value (at the start of the period) for a portfolio, and
R$_i$ is the rate of return for portfolio "i."

Or alternatively:

$$C = \frac{\Sigma(MVB_i \times R_i)}{MVB_{TOTAL}}$$

The composite returns should be calculated at least quarterly (monthly is preferred). If monthly composite returns are calculated, the monthly returns are linked geometrically using this formula:

$$C_{QT} = (1 + C_{MO_1})(1 + C_{MO_2})(1 + C_{MO_3}) - 1$$

where C_{QT} is the composite quarterly return, and
C_{MO_1}, C_{MO_2}, and C_{MO_3} are the composite returns for months 1, 2, and 3, respectively.

Similarly, to compute the annual rate of return for composite returns calculated quarterly, use the formula:

$$C_Y = (1 + C_{Q1})(1 + C_{Q2})(1 + C_{Q3})(1 + C_{Q4}) - 1$$

where C_{Q1}, C_{Q2}, C_{Q3}, and C_{Q4} are composite returns for quarters 1, 2, 3, and 4, respectively.

Valuation Periods and Weighting. The standards require that beginning-of-period market values be used to weight the portfolio returns in a composite. End-of-period values present a consistent upward bias in performance, because better-performing portfolios would always have a greater weight in the composite return.

If portfolios are valued quarterly, each portfolio's return is weighted by the beginning-of-quarter market value for the portfolio in computing the quarterly composite. If portfolios are valued monthly and linked to get the quarterly return, the return is calculated using either of the two following approaches:
- Compute the size-weighted composite return for each month, and link these monthly returns to get the quarterly return. This approach is more precise and so is preferred.

- Link the (unweighted) monthly returns to get the quarterly return for each portfolio. Then weight each portfolio using its beginning-of-quarter market value, and compute the asset-weighted composite return.

An even more precise value can be obtained by using the asset- and cash-flow-weighted method.

Methods for Allocating Cash. The standards require that cash be allocated to the segment returns of a multiple-asset portfolio when the segment returns are being presented as evidence of ability to manage the segment by itself. The standards require that cash be allocated in a way that is representative of a manager's intended style. Characteristics common to an acceptable method are:

- The method must allow for an *ex ante* decision to allocate cash.
- The method must meet the tests of being reasonable and representative.
- The method should allow for an audit trail that provides evidence of the cash allocation decision.

As of January 1, 1993, this cash allocation must be made at the beginning of the reporting period. Several different methods may be used.

The *separate portfolios approach* involves simply splitting the multiple-asset funds into separate portfolios based on asset class. The portfolios may be merged for client reporting and may be measured separately for performance purposes. This method is conceptually simple and is available on some portfolio management systems with no modifications. A disadvantage is that separate portfolios increase the workload involved in portfolio administration by increasing the number of portfolios that must be managed. The approach also means that the money market management function is made more complicated by the increased number of portfolios that must be traded.

The *multiple cash balances approach* involves maintaining separate cash balances for the segments within a single multiple-asset portfolio. In this method, the original number of portfolios is maintained. But the extra effort involved in administration differs little from the separate portfolios approach. Short-term trading must still be segregated by asset class, and cash transactions have to be entered to move cash from one segment to another. A decision matrix must be maintained to direct which cash balance will be affected by each of the various transaction types. Problems of interpretation can also arise in international trading where, for example, a German asset is settled in U.S. dollars.

Finally, the *allocation of cash returns approach* involves the allocation of rates of return rather than the maintenance of actual separate cash balances.

Under this approach, cash and equivalents is maintained as a single entity in the multiple-asset portfolio. The rate of return for cash and equivalents and for all the asset segments is determined. The cash and equivalents returns are then allocated to the segment returns to create segment-plus-cash returns.

This approach has a minimal impact on current management and administration practices. There is no need to segregate short-term trading by asset class, increase the number of portfolios, or develop a decision matrix for the cash effects of trading.

The tests of reasonableness and representativeness are to be determined by the individual money manager in light of a particular investment strategy. The determination of the appropriate method for allocating cash returns will be determined on a case-by-case basis.

There are at least two methods of allocating cash returns:

- *Predetermined cash allocation mix applied to residual cash.* At the beginning of the reporting period, the manager sets a cash allocation mix (e.g., 60 percent stocks, 40 percent bonds); residual cash is allocated accordingly. This approach is appropriate for strategies that call for nearly 100 percent investment at all times—that is, the effect of residual cash has minimal impact on the single-asset results.

- *Cash allocation based on target asset class percentages determined at the beginning of the period.* Actual asset allocations are compared to the beginning-of-period target allocations. If a segment is underinvested relative to its beginning-of-period target, the differential is drawn from residual cash plus cash equivalents, and the appropriate cash return is applied. If a segment is overinvested, no adjustment is made.

Actual asset allocations are compared to the beginning-of period target allocations. If a segment is underinvested relative to its beginning-of-period target, the differential is drawn from residual cash and cash equivalents. If a segment is overinvested relative to its beginning-of-period target, the segment borrows from cash and cash equivalents; the borrowing cost is the cash segment return (cash and cash equivalents). This borrowing cost is deducted from the single-asset return. There is the possibility of a negative cash balance with this approach. It might also imply that the investment strategy uses leverage.

Also, actual asset allocations may be compared to the beginning-of-period target allocations with the addition of the return weights being adjusted by purchases, sales, contributions, withdrawals, and income. According to this method, the target allocations are readjusted to reflect active allocation decisions by the manager throughout the period.

Finally, borrowing also may occur between segments in addition to the cash segment. If an asset segment is underinvested, assets are allocated to meet the beginning-of-period target. If residual cash was insufficient, however, borrowing occurs between the other segments. Instead of using a blended return of segment plus cash and cash equivalents, the manager applies blended returns based on segment returns. Overweighted segments borrow at a segment cost, and underinvested segments are mixed with segment returns rather than with the cash return. This approach might be representative if bonds are used as equity surrogates and vice versa.

Retroactive Cash Allocation

The characteristics of *ex ante* decision making and the provision of an audit trail must be replicated for retroactive cash allocation. Unless a manager can identify a method that accurately represents what the historical cash allocation would have been, retroactive cash allocation should not be attempted.

APPENDIX B
MEASURES OF RISK AND DISPERSION

To provide a fuller understanding of risk measures that might be used to meet the recommendations of the standards, this appendix sets forth several examples, including comments and recommended treatment for performance presentation. External and internal risk measures both should be considered in presenting performance results. External risk measures evaluate the riskiness of investment strategies. Measures of this kind, based on current and historical data, can be used to project the future riskiness of a strategy. Internal risk measures are techniques that evaluate how consistently a manager performs with respect to individual portfolios within a composite.

External Risk Measures—Investment Strategy Risk

There is a trade-off between risk and return. A manager who earned 15 percent is not necessarily better than a manager who earned 14 percent if the former took more risk than the latter. A number of methods can be used to measure the riskiness of alternative strategies.

Standard Deviation. Standard deviation of portfolio performance over time (S_p) is a measure of volatility. It indicates how far data spread about their central tendency or mean. The standard deviation of historical data for an asset-weighted composite over time is calculated as follows:[1]

$$S_p = \sqrt{\frac{\sum[C_{ASSET_i} - MEAN(C_{ASSET})]^2}{n}}$$

---

1. The use of n in the denominator of standard deviation (as opposed to $n-1$) is supported because using n yields the maximum likelihood estimate of standard deviation. The use of $n-1$ in the denominator of sample variance makes sample variance, s^2, an unbiased estimate of the true variance, σ^2. However, when the square root of s^2 is taken to get the sample standard deviation, s, the result is not an unbiased estimate of population standard deviation, σ. The seldom-used unbiased estimate of standard deviation has a cumbersome constant based on sample size, which needs to be calculated. Because the unbiased estimate of standard deviation is not practical, it is wise to use the maximum likelihood estimate of standard deviation.

    Further compounding the issue is the fact that the use of $n-1$ (unbiased) hinges on the assumptions that random and independent samples are taken from a normal distribution. The sample data (in this case, the manager's returns) are not random, arguably not independent, and may not be normally distributed.

Association for Investment Management and Research

where C_{ASSET_i} is the asset-weighted composite return in the *i*th time period, and

n is the number of periods in the study.

In theory, a portfolio that is more volatile than an index or benchmark should receive a higher return in exchange for taking extra risk. When looking at investment strategy risk, one tends to use the past to project forward. For example, it is reasonable to assume that a manager's strategy will continue to display the same volatility or risk level in the future as it has historically. The use of standard deviation in gauging the riskiness of a strategy is consistent with the use of this statistic in measuring historical volatility as a predictor of the riskiness of an asset class, although the measure is subject to time period selection bias. Understanding some of the limitations of standard deviation as a measure of volatility can help an investor use this well-accepted and important statistic.

Beta. Beta is the average performance volatility relative to the market. Some clients with a long-term perspective feel that high volatility is not necessarily bad in that it may well be rewarded by excess return over time. Most agree, however, that given two identical sets of returns, they prefer the one that was achieved in the more consistent manner. In assessing the *ex ante* market volatility of a single portfolio at a specific time, there are many possible definitions of beta—weighted actual stock returns over the previous 60 months, up markets versus down markets, exponential weighting to place greater weight on recent time periods, etc. The beta referred to in the standards, however, pertains to the history of a group of portfolios, not the current holdings.

This *ex post* definition of beta is calculated as the coefficient of a least squares linear regression of composite performance (either monthly or quarterly as far back as possible) relative to a broad index of market performance (usually the S&P 500, but managers might well justify a different index as being more appropriate to their style). A simple regression for such a characteristic line uses absolute returns. A slightly more complicated but more correct form was proposed by Sharpe as the Capital Asset Pricing Model and by Jensen for portfolios. In this case, the equation is defined in terms of excess returns:

$$Y - R_f = \alpha + \beta (X - R_f)$$

where Y = manager composite performance;
X = index performance;

α = regression intercept;
β = regression coefficient or slope; and
R_f = the risk-free return during the period, usually defined as the 90-day Treasury bill return, but a manager might justifiably use a longer maturity.

In either case, the best linear fit of composite performance to the index can be calculated as

$$\beta = \frac{\Sigma(X \times Y)}{\Sigma X^2}$$

$$\alpha = \bar{Y} - \beta \times \bar{X}$$

where $\bar{Y}$ = the average of all months of composite performance (or excess performance adjusted for the risk-free rate) and $\bar{X}$ = the average of all months of index performance (or excess performance).

The Sharpe Measure. The Sharpe measure (SM_p) is a ratio defined as the excess return on a portfolio divided by the volatility of the securities. Its formula is as follows:

$$SM_p = \frac{(\text{Composite Performance} - R_f)}{S_p}$$

where R_f is the risk-free rate of interest, and
S_p is the standard deviation of the portfolio.

The ratio is a measure of reward relative to total volatility. It may be used to assist an investor to determine how much risk will maximize his or her utility. A large portfolio of securities should receive some reward for taking on volatility (s_p); otherwise, it would be sensible to have a portfolio of Treasury bills. As a result, the Sharpe measure, which uses total volatility, seems to be most useful when the portfolio being evaluated represents all of an investor's marketable assets. The Sharpe measure for the portfolio can be compared to the Sharpe measure for the benchmark.

The Treynor Measure. The Treynor measure (TM_p) is a ratio defined as the excess return on a portfolio divided by the portfolio's average beta. Its

$$TM_p = (\text{Composite Performance} - R_f) / \beta_p$$

The ratio is a measure of reward relative to total systematic volatility, or relative risk. The riskiness of individual securities or a small group of securities may best be described by their comovement with the market (β). As a result, the Treynor measure seems to be particularly useful when the investor's portfolio is one of many portfolios included in a large investment fund. The Treynor measure for the portfolio can be compared to the Treynor measure for the benchmark.

The comparison ratios introduced by Sharpe and Treynor have important implications if one recognizes the weaknesses of the primary risk statistics, namely standard deviation and beta. The bottom line is that no one statistic can consistently capture the riskiness of an asset class or a style of management. The use of a variety of measures with an understanding of their shortcomings will provide the most valuable information.

Composites versus Benchmarks

Benchmarks are used to make comparisons in risk and return. Benchmarks can include a variety of alternatives such as market indexes, manager universes, and normal portfolios. Each type of benchmark has advantages and disadvantages. A brief explanation of each is provided. The risk measures described above are often reviewed on a relative basis compared to one or more benchmarks.

Indexes. The most commonly employed benchmark for an investment strategy is a market index. Indexes are viewed as "an independent representation of the market" and are generally readily available. Examples of standardized market indexes include the S&P 500, Wilshire 5000, and the Russell 2000 in the equity market; the Lehman Brothers Government/Corporate or Aggregate, Salomon Brothers Broad, or Merrill Lynch Master in the fixed-income market; and the Russell Commercial Real Estate in the real estate market. In addition to a wide variety of standardized indexes, customized indexes can be created to reflect a specific strategy and a universe of securities. Further, indexes can be mixed to represent an allocation among markets. Although indexes are widely utilized and can offer significant insight regarding relative risk, there is significant potential for misinterpretation when an index does not accurately reflect the strategy or universe of securities employed. Indexes implicitly assume cost-free transactions. Some assume reinvestment of income.

Manager Universes. Consultants gather data on styles of investment management to create a "universe" of return data. These universes have the potential to match styles more effectively than do simple indexes, although there are some problems in implementation. The problems include different managers conforming to different reporting procedures, completeness and accuracy of data, sample size for specialty strategies, and survivor bias. Although problems exist, universes remain an important part of measuring relative risk and return.

Normal Portfolios. A "normal portfolio" is a specially designed benchmark portfolio that controls for investment strategy and therefore provides a bogey for evaluating discretionary investment decisions. Although normal portfolios are not used extensively in the industry at this time, they offer a valuable means to judge specific risk. Unfortunately, normal portfolios also suffer from being generally difficult to construct and maintain. They seem to work better as a specific client's benchmark rather than as a strategy comparison.

When judging the various approaches for measuring risk, a more thorough investigation of these techniques and measures is recommended in addition to a review of other measures that have been proposed and utilized over the years. The individual investment strategy should determine the best benchmark or combination of benchmarks. Obviously, an index strategy must be compared to the appropriate index. A low-price–earnings fund, because there is a large enough population of similar strategies and no simple index available for comparison, might best be judged against an appropriate manager universe. Because active balanced managers may differ substantially in their approaches, their risk may best be judged against a very specific normal portfolio. The standards strongly recommend the use of consistently applied risk measures appropriate to a given strategy to provide a complete picture of performance.

Internal Risk Measures

Most of the literature about the riskiness of a management style or strategy centers on the external measures of risk for evaluating a manager's performance composite on an absolute basis or as compared to a target benchmark. Far less effort has been expended on determining how consistently a manager applies that strategy across portfolios within a composite. The fact that an investment professional, on average, earned 10 percent last year is of little comfort to the client who actually earned 2 percent within the context of the same strategy. Dispersion within a composite is a relevant and valuable piece of information for an investor.

Regardless of the approach to averaging, the use of composites for aggregating results calls for some measure to gauge the consistency of those results. Traditionally, the range of returns and standard deviation have been the commonly used methods. These statistics have advantages and disadvantages. The introduction of asset-weighting creates some problems with using traditional standard deviation as a meaningful statistic. An alternative is to use a generalized reformulation of standard deviation. This asset-weighted dispersion measure will be discussed, as well as other measures that may provide insights into the dispersion of results within a composite.

Standard Deviation. The most widely accepted measure of dispersion within a composite is standard deviation across equal-weighted portfolios (S_c). The definition is as follows:

$$S_c = \sqrt{\frac{\Sigma[R_i - MEAN(R)]^2}{n}}$$

where R_i is the return on the ith portfolio, and
n is the number of portfolios.

This definition assumes a normally distributed population and should therefore be applied to an equal-weighted composite.

Tables B-1 and B-2 contain examples that illustrate some problems with using equal-weighted composites and "traditional" standard deviation. The example shows two similar managers, with identical asset-weighted means of 17.5 percent within their respective composites. However, Manager One has an equal-weighted composite of 12.5 percent, while Manager Two has an equal-weighted composite of 17.5 percent. Because both managers have shown an equal level of skill, it can be argued that they should have similar means and dispersion statistics, because each turned $200,000 into $235,000 (10 percent on $100,000 and 25 percent on $100,000) in the same fashion. The example shows the shortcomings inherent in using equal-weighted composites and deviations.

These two managers should have the same measure of dispersion; that is, their dollars are equally clustered around their asset-weighted average of 17.5 percent.

Table B-1. Equal-Weighted Example

Portfolio	Return	Capitalization	$[R_i - MEAN(R)]^2$
Manager One			
A	10%	$20,000	.000625
B	10	20,000	.000625
C	10	20,000	.000625
D	10	20,000	.000625
E	10	20,000	.000625
F	25	100,000	.015625
Composite return			12.50%
Standard deviation			5.59%
Manager Two			
A	10	100,000	.005625
B	25	100,000	.005625
Composite return			17.50%
Standard deviation			7.50%

Table B-2. Asset-Weighted Example

Portfolio	Return	Capitalization	$w_i(R_i - C_{ASSET})^2$
Manager One			
A	10%	$ 20,000	(20/200) × (.005625)
B	10	20,000	(20/200) × (.005625)
C	10	20,000	(20/200) × (.005625)
D	10	20,000	(20/200) × (.005625)
E	10	20,000	(20/200) × (.005625)
F	25	100,000	(100/200) × (.005625)
Composite return			17.50%
Standard deviation			7.50%
Manager Two			
A	10	100,000	(100/200) × (.005625)
B	25	100,000	(100/200) × (.005625)
Composite return			17.50%
Standard deviation			7.50%

To create a dispersion measure that explains deviation from the asset-weighted composite is relatively straightforward. The formulation begins with the calculation from an asset-weighted mean. The asset-weighted composite return is formulated as follows:

$$C_{ASSET} = \frac{\Sigma MVB_i \times R_i}{MVB_{TOTAL}}$$

where MVB_i is the market value of the ith portfolio in the composite at the beginning of the period, and
R_i is the unweighted return on the ith portfolio.

The reformulation of standard deviation to achieve a meaningful statistic to apply to an asset-weighted mean is as follows:

$$\text{Dispersion} = \sqrt{\Sigma w_i(R_i - C_{ASSET})^2}$$

where w_i is the weight of the ith portfolio or (MVB_i/MVB_{TOTAL}).

Importantly, an asset-weighted composite does not measure the performance of the average portfolio. It measures the performance of the average dollar. An asset-weighted composite can be thought of as the performance of one dollar, had that dollar been invested in every client's portfolio in proportion to the weight of the client's portfolio within the composite.

The traditional standard deviation from an equal-weighted mean is merely a special case of standard deviation from an asset-weighted mean. One of the problems with many measures of dispersion is that there are no standardized units. Standard deviation within a composite uses percent.

Unlike rates of return, standard deviation and the proposed asset-weighted dispersion measure cannot be annualized. Log-normal, continuously compounded rates of return have standard deviations that can be annualized in a simple fashion. Deviations from asset-weighted or equal-weighted means cannot be annualized. The calculation of an annual dispersion statistic requires annual rate-of-return data. To calculate quarterly and monthly dispersion, quarterly and monthly data are required. Although this requirement can be proved algebraically, an intuitive example will show why the deviations cannot be linked. Table B-3 assumes there are no transactions on accounts that begin the year with $1 million. For the year, this manager has zero deviation, yet there has been dispersion along the way. The numbers themselves are only

Table B-3. Asset-Weighted Deviation Example

Period	Client A	Client B	Asset-Weighted Deviation
Q1	2.00%	0.00%	1.00%
Q2	8.00	0.00	4.00
Q3	−3.00	8.00	5.49
Q4	0.00	−1.06	0.53
Year	6.86	6.86	0.00

relevant within their time frame. (The results are nearly identical for equal-weighted returns.)

Additionally, there is no value in averaging 4 quarters of data for some kind of "quarterly average." To take these numbers and divide them by 4 has no mathematical relevance.

High–Low and Range. The high–low and range are the simplest and most easily understood measures of dispersion. Their key advantages are simplicity, ease of calculation, and ease of interpretation. On the downside, one extreme value could skew the appearance of the data. By itself, the calculation of the high–low and the range of returns, which will be the same for equal-weighted and asset-weighted composites, is not particularly rigorous. However, coupling these measures with other measures, such as the one shown below, increases the value of presenting the high–low and range of returns.

Quartile Dollar Dispersion (QDD). High–low and range by themselves are not adequate measures of risk because, like standard deviation, they are prone to extreme values that may skew the picture. Therefore, it would be helpful to consider alternative measures of dispersion. The following example uses the spread of dollars across quartiles to provide additional insights into the dispersion of returns. Note that even though a portfolio is broken into quartiles, this measure has nothing to do with quartiles for returns shown in manager universes.

Using the data in Table B-4, the rate of return on different quartiles can be calculated. For example, for the worst-performing 25 percent,

$$QDD4 = \frac{200,000}{250,000}(.08) + \frac{50,000}{250,000}(.09) = 8.2 \text{ percent}$$

42 Appendix B

Table B-4. QDD Example: Data

Portfolio	Return	Capitalization
A	8%	$200,000
B	9	200,000
C	10	400,000
D	11	100,000
E	15	100,000

The rate of return on the best-performing quartile is

$$QDD1 = \frac{100,000}{250,000}(.15) + \frac{100,000}{250,000}(.11) + \frac{50,000}{250,000}(.10)$$
$$= 12.4 \text{ percent}$$

QDD is not prone to the extremes because it covers one-fourth of the data in both directions. At the same time, it gives the client a feel for the data.

Sample Report

Table B-5 provides a sample report showing return and selected risk measures. Additionally, a manager should have the option of supplementing (not substituting) this table with equal-weighted composites and standard deviations from an equal-weighted mean.

Table B-5. Sample Dispersion Report

Period	Asset-Weighted Mean	Highest Performer	QDD1	QDD4	Lowest Performer	Asset-Weighted Dispersion
Year	10.00%	15.00%	12.40%	8.20%	8.00%	1.90%
Q1	4.10	6.00	5.20	3.20	3.00	0.83
Q2	0.50	2.00	1.41	−0.80	−1.00	0.92
Q3	−1.29	0.00	0.24	−2.00	−2.00	0.60
Q4	6.52	8.03	7.78	5.76	5.72	0.88

Measures of risk should be designed to provide information to the client and the potential client. The best measures have the following properties:

Association for Investment Management and Research

- There should be no way for a manager to manipulate the measure to his or her advantage.
- The measure should be relatively easy to interpret. The mathematical power of a measure matters little unless it can be calculated and interpreted with relative ease.
- It should apply in a uniform fashion to managers of all sizes.

APPENDIX C
INTERNATIONAL INVESTMENTS

This appendix provides additional information on the requirements, disclosures, and recommendations that are specifically pertinent to international investments.

Performance Calculations

AIMR recommends the use of trade-date rather than settlement-date reporting. The volatility of the different equity and currency markets plus the lengthy settlement periods in some countries make the issue of trade-date versus settlement-date reporting particularly important for international portfolios.

Foreign taxes that may be recoverable on financial transactions by a foreign investor, depending on tax status and national treaties, present a performance problem unique to international investors. Portfolio returns should be calculated net of withholding taxes on dividends, interest, and capital gains. Comparison benchmarks may be shown gross (no withholding taxes taken) or net (after withholding taxes); if net, the amount of taxes withheld should reflect the perspective of the client or prospective client. Recognizing that net indexes are easier to outperform than gross indexes, presentations must disclose whether the benchmark is gross or net of taxes; if net, the assumed tax rate must be disclosed. Net performance should be calculated after subtracting potential capital gains taxes on unrealized gains when applicable, particularly in emerging markets. If this is not done, perhaps because taxes are only required after funds are taken out of the country, then disclosure of the percentage of the portfolio involved is recommended. Further discussion of benchmarks and foreign taxes on financial transactions is included in the last section of this appendix, "Gross versus Net Dividend Benchmarks."

Conversion of a benchmark and a portfolio into the base currency should be carried out using the same exchange rates, if possible. If this is not possible, note should be made of any significant deviations—for example, when the market and/or points in time used for pricing currencies are different among portfolios. (Note: Base currency refers to the currency of the country in which the investor is based; for example, for a U.S.-based investor, the base currency would be U.S. dollars. Local currency refers to the currency of the country of interest; for example, yen would be the local currency for the Japanese component of a portfolio.) Managers may choose which exchange rates to use to convert performance.

Association for Investment Management and Research

Construction of Composites

As is the case for domestic portfolios, no absolute rules govern when to include or exclude portfolios from a composite. Managers of international portfolios must be the final judges of which portfolios belong in a composite and when restrictions are likely to render a portfolio unrepresentative of a particular style. For example, some managers make portfolio country-weighting decisions based upon a published index. In this case, portfolios running against different indexes—one weighted by gross domestic product versus one weighted by capitalization, for example—belong in separate composites because the country weightings will be different. A manager who tends not to change portfolio construction based on the benchmark might have only one global composite. Portfolios must not be moved in and out of composites except for valid changes in investment objectives or constraints. Consequently, the decision to include or exclude a multicountry portfolio in a certain composite is important, and the implications of all constraints should be considered carefully.

Composites, however defined, must be compared to benchmarks that parallel the risk or investment styles that the client portfolios are expected to track. For composites that are defined relative to a benchmark (e.g., portfolios managed against the EAFE), disclosure of the percentage of the portfolio invested in countries not contained in the benchmark is required; disclosure of the range or average of country weights is recommended.

The following are some examples of the types of rules managers could use when constructing composites of international portfolios:

- Balanced portfolios with differing asset mixes (e.g., 60 percent equity/40 percent bond versus 40 percent equity/60 percent bond).
- Portfolios with different benchmarks (e.g., EAFE versus EAFE ex Japan). Investment restrictions can vary greatly from client to client. A practical and objective way to deal with this problem is to specify a level of constraint on the portfolio for composite membership. For example, a manager could define a composite as portfolios that have global investment objectives and constraints excluding less than 5 percent of the benchmark. This would allow inclusion of portfolios that cannot invest in one or two small countries, if the manager believes that the portfolios are representative of the composite's style.
- Portfolios with different levels of constraints relative to the same benchmark. Portfolios that are constrained as to how far their portfolio composition can deviate from the benchmark weightings may not belong in the same composite as portfolios that are completely uncon-

strained. For example, portfolios that are limited in how far their country weights are allowed to deviate from the index weights might be unrepresentative of a style that leads to large differences in country weightings compared to the benchmark.
- Portfolios that invest a large portion of their assets in countries outside the benchmark (e.g., emerging markets). These might be kept in a composite separate from portfolios that invest only in countries included in the benchmark. A stated minimum percentage invested in benchmark countries may be useful in defining the composite.

Managers are encouraged to develop their own objective criteria for constructing composites. Clear and detailed definitions of composites are necessary, particularly for multicountry portfolios.

As with the domestic composites, the calculation and display of measures of dispersion for portfolio returns within a composite (high–low portfolio returns in the composite, range of returns, or an asset-weighted dispersion measure) for each time period is recommended.

The Creation of Stand-Alone Composites

The creation of stand-alone composites from subsectors or carve-outs of larger international portfolios is only in compliance if these subsectors were actually managed as separate entities with their own cash allocations and currency management. Results for a subsector or carve-out that was not treated as a separate entity must be presented as supplemental information to the composite or composites from which the carve-out was drawn. This requirement is stricter than the similar subsector requirements for domestic portfolios because of:
- difficulties in assigning cash to the subsectors of multicurrency portfolios,
- difficulties in assigning results of currency-hedging strategies to subsectors when the hedging strategy is designed for the portfolio as a whole,
- the potential impact of currency-hedging strategies on the subsector's asset allocation (i.e., the subsector represents an unhedged portion of the portfolio that is not representative of how the subsector would have been managed had currency hedging been allowed), and
- differences in diversification properties for the securities held as a small portion of a larger account as compared to securities held in a stand-alone portfolio.

Association for Investment Management and Research

The manager must disclose if the stand-alone composite is a subset or carve-out from a larger composite, and if so, the subsector's assets as a percentage of the larger composite is also required.

If a stand-alone composite is formed using subsectors drawn from multiple composites, its return must be presented with a list of the underlying composites from which the subsector was drawn, along with the percentage of each composite the subsector represents. Performance for each of the larger composites must be made available to prospective clients. Although the inclusion in the subsector or carve-out of all qualifying portfolios is preferred, the presentation of subsector results as supplemental information may be based on representative portfolios as long as this is disclosed.

Attribution

The inclusion of attribution as supplementary information in presentations is encouraged. Because different methodologies for calculating attribution can lead to different results, attribution analysis should be accompanied by a clear explanation of the methodology used.

Hedged and Unhedged Portfolios

If a composite is to be compared to an unhedged benchmark, portfolios that are allowed to use currency hedging should not be included with portfolios that cannot use hedging instruments, unless the use of currency hedging is judged to be immaterial. Similarly, if portfolios managed against hedged benchmarks are materially different from portfolios managed against unhedged benchmarks, they should be placed in separate composites.

Returns Excluding the Effect of Currency

When expressing the return of a portfolio excluding the effect of currency, the return should be shown fully hedged back to the base currency of that portfolio. This is because the investor cannot actually achieve the local return of a market that is denominated in a currency different from the portfolio's base currency, whereas the hedged return is possible. If this hedged return is not calculated, disclosure must be made that the return is in the local currency and does not account for interest rate differentials in forward currency exchange rates.

The total return from currency can be closely approximated by taking the percentage (i.e., geometric difference) between the total return in base currency and the total return in local currency, although a more accurate method is to take the percentage difference between the total in base currency and the total fully hedged into base currency, if this is available.

Currency Overlay Portfolios

There are four broad categories of currency overlay portfolios:

- *Portfolios whose objectives are to add value and/or control risk relative to the unhedged (by the overlay manager) portfolio.* The objective might be to achieve a positive gain from hedging relative to zero or, alternatively, a total currency return (combining the returns from the currency exposure of the underlying assets with the returns from hedging) in excess of zero.

- *Portfolios for which the benchmark is the underlying assets of the portfolio hedged back to a base currency in some proportion.* The benchmarks of portfolios in this category have a predetermined, fixed-percentage exposure in the base currency; for example, a "50 percent hedged into U.S. dollars" benchmark has an overall dollar exposure of 50 percent. If the underlying portfolio already has U.S. dollars via exposure to the U.S. equity market, for example, then it is possible that no hedging would be required to calculate the benchmark, because the dollar exposure may already be 50 percent. It may even be necessary to "sell" some dollars to calculate the benchmark. If the benchmark does require further hedging to achieve its 50 percent dollar exposure, however, the benchmark is calculated such that the same proportion of each currency is sold.

- *Portfolios with asset-based benchmarks.* These are similar to the previous category, but for the same "50 percent hedged into U.S. dollars" example, 50 percent of all nondollar currencies are sold into U.S. dollars regardless of the U.S dollar exposure already inherent in the underlying assets. So the benchmark may well have a U.S. dollar exposure greater than 50 percent.

- *Portfolios whose benchmarks are published, either specifically for a portfolio or generally.* An example is the currency return of MSCI EAFE 100 percent hedged into U.S. dollars.

Returns on currency overlay portfolios should be calculated whenever there are notified changes in the underlying exposures (as the result of a shift in the underlying assets). This means that whenever the overlay manager receives notification of change in the underlying assets (e.g., revaluation of assets from the custodian), all the contracts should be revalued. In accordance with the overall presentation standards, currency overlay portfolios must be valued at least quarterly; however, the volatile nature of these portfolios may make the use of shorter time periods necessary to obtain full and fair disclosure.

Two portfolios with the same benchmark may apply different mandates to the overlay portfolio managers. For example, for cases when the mandates are based on the underlying assets, the return of the overlay performance benchmark will be different unless the underlying assets of two portfolios imply identical currency exposures. Consequently, the performance benchmark for any currency overlay portfolio must be calculated in accordance with the mandate of the portfolio (unless the benchmark is actually the currency return on a published benchmark).

In terms of currency exposure, composites should be determined according to similar benchmarks and restrictions. In currency management, the underlying currency exposure might not matter if portfolios are managed according to similar benchmarks. If, however, the manager is being measured according to the value added over the existing positions, then the underlying currency exposure becomes critical. In this case, grouping currency overlay portfolios into composites of more than one portfolio would not be meaningful. A series of one-portfolio composites is recommended when composites of multiple-currency overlay portfolios does not provide useful information to prospective clients. A list of all such composites must be made available.

Total returns of the composite and the benchmark must be shown on the same basis. Each composite's return should be accompanied by any relevant information regarding restrictions—target benchmark, no cross-hedging, no net short positions, and so on.

Benchmark Reporting: Gross versus Net of Withholding Taxes

The standards recommend calculation of portfolio returns net of withholding taxes on dividends, interest, and capital gains. Some comparison benchmarks are published on a "gross" and on a "net" basis. "Gross" refers to a total return including capital appreciation plus income (monthly dividend yield). "Net" refers to a gross return with interest or dividend income on a "net of withholding taxes" basis. Managers must disclose whether composite and benchmark returns are net of foreign withholding taxes and must disclose the assumed withholding tax rate used to calculate a net benchmark total return. Benchmark on a net basis from the base currency withholding tax perspective will be an easier and more appropriate bogey to be measured against.

The United States has tax treaties with many countries. U.S. investors receive tax credits from the U.S. government for taxes paid. Tax-exempt investors frequently receive withheld tax from foreign governments. There should be no U.S. withholding tax for domestic-based pension funds. The effects of withholding taxes will vary depending upon the investor's base country.

The MSCI Net Dividend Indexes, among the most widely used, assume the most conservative tax perspective, that of a Luxembourg holding company. Luxembourg has few tax treaties, and Luxembourg-based investors pay the maximum of dividend taxes. Ideally, calculation of net indexes should be from the tax perspective of the client. Calculation of net indexes from each perspective, however, could be complex because of data limitations. Over the 23 years ending on December 31, 1992, the MSCI Luxembourg-based EAFE Index on a gross total return basis rose an annualized 12.65 percent compared with an 11.72 percent return provided on a net basis in U.S. dollar terms.

A widely used methodology for calculating monthly net-of-dividend tax benchmarks is:

$$\{(\text{Current Price Index}/\text{Previous Price Index}) \times [(\text{Current Monthly Yield}/100) \times (1 - \text{Withholding Tax \%}) + 1] - 1\} \times 100$$

Table C-1 provides an illustration of this calculation.

Table C-1. Return to Australian Portfolio in U.S. Dollars

Current price index	201.466
Previous price index	210.936
Annualized yield	4.2
Monthly yield	.35
Withholding tax	30%
Published returns	
Price	−4.49
Net	−4.25

Calculation:
$$\left(\frac{201.466}{210.936} \times \left[\frac{.35}{100} \times (1-.30) + 1\right] - 1\right) \times 100 = -4.25\%$$

The handling of income in some international indexes (including the MSCI indexes) is imprecise because income is applied monthly as one-twelfth of the annual dividend yield rather than accounting for the dividends as they are received.

Some fixed-income portfolio benchmarks are calculated net of withholding taxes. As with equity portfolios, the actual impact of taxes depends on the investor's home country. For example, U.S.-based investors are subject to a 10 percent withholding tax in Japan, while Japan-based investors are not subject to that tax. The same "net" benchmark could not be used for both investors. Currently, Salomon Brothers offers its aggregate and component global bond indexes net of taxes from a U.S.-based pension plan perspective.

APPENDIX D
EXAMPLES OF PORTFOLIOS USING LEVERAGE AND/OR DERIVATIVE SECURITIES

To provide a fuller understanding of the recommended procedures in the standards for dealing with portfolios using leverage and/or derivatives, this appendix sets forth several examples, including comments and recommended treatment for performance presentation.

For purposes of this discussion, two universally accepted definitions of leverage in the investment context, referred to as the accounting and the economic definitions, will be used. Each is appropriate in some cases. An *accountant* would say that leverage results when total assets are greater than net assets, i.e., whenever some part of the assets are financed by liabilities or borrowing. An *economist* (or perhaps a portfolio manager) would say that leverage results when the return from a portfolio is expected to be proportionately more volatile than the return from a benchmark (unleveraged) portfolio.

Leverage: Example Scenarios

The following six examples illustrate that leverage can occur without derivatives through margin-buying or short-selling, and that derivatives need not give rise to leverage nor necessitate restating to an all-cash basis.

Example 1: A manager is given $5,000 to invest in securities on behalf of an account. The manager purchases $10,000 in stocks on margin. This portfolio is leveraged in both the accounting and economic senses. The $10,000 purchase exceeds the $5,000 investment because of the borrowing of $5,000 for margin. Also, the portfolio must achieve roughly twice the return of a portfolio for which the manager held $5,000 in the same stocks without borrowing (adjusted for borrowing cost).

Comment: Few people would dispute that this example uses leverage. Moreover, the restatement to an all-cash basis is fairly straightforward and would use the actual accounting records for the transactions involved (purchase of stock, borrowing of margin, payment of margin interest, etc.). This restatement goes to all cash by recasting the portfolio to appear as though it were $10,000, not $5,000.

Recommendation: Disclosure of the portfolio as being leveraged is required, with whatever additional information about the use of leverage thoroughly discussed. The all-cash return must be computed and disclosed.

The principle that requires the all-cash restatement is that buying stocks is possible on an all-cash basis, and the portfolio could have bought the same stocks at the same prices if it actually had the cash to do so. The computation of the all-cash return, R_{AC}, is as follows:

$$R_{AC} = \frac{MVE + Interest_{MARGIN}}{MVB}$$

where MVE is the total market value of the assets at the end of the period;
MVB is the total market value of the assets at the beginning of the period, including the margin borrowing; and
$Interest_{MARGIN}$ is the margin interest expense during the period.

The margin interest is added back to the total asset value because, under the assumption of all cash, the portfolio would not have incurred the expense of borrowing.

Any increase (decrease) of margin debt during the period must be treated as cash flow to the total assets, because such an increase (decrease) to margin debt occurs concurrently with an identical increase (decrease) in total assets. All other requirements and guidelines related to calculating time-weighted total returns, revaluation of the portfolio for cash flows, etc., must be applied. It is not recommended that this portfolio be included in an unleveraged equity composite, because the portfolio has a higher degree of risk than an unleveraged portfolio.

Example 2: A manager purchases $10 million in an S&P Index fund and buys $10 million in S&P 500 stock index futures for an account.

Comment: This portfolio must be viewed as leveraged, as opposed to being considered an equity portfolio with a beta of 2.0. Any restatement of the return to an all-cash basis would recast the portfolio as though it were $20 million. The principle that requires the all-cash restatement is that it would be possible to get the same leverage by borrowing $10 million and buying the stocks, making the portfolio look like the portfolio in Example 1. Because the portfolio in Example 1 can and must be restated to an all-cash basis, the portfolio in Example 2 must likewise be restated. Consider what it would mean to calculate the incremental return as the difference between the total fund return and the fund return without derivatives. The equity portfolio is most likely managed with the objective of being a competitive equity portfolio in its own right. The futures are probably not part of the equity management strategy itself but instead are likely intended to meet other strategic objectives such as asset allocation, market timing, or hedging other assets not in the portfolio. Thus, without further disclosure of the purpose of the futures, it is probably not meaningful nor representative to calculate the incremental return because of the use of the futures.

Recommendation: Disclosure of the portfolio as being leveraged is required, with whatever additional information about the use of the futures and leverage thoroughly discussed. The all-cash return must be computed and disclosed. Because futures prices incorporate imputed borrowing costs, the method of computing the all-cash return is consistent with that proposed for the portfolio in Example 1. The all-cash return would be the ending total portfolio value, including the ending futures value, divided by $20 million.

Example 3: A manager has used an account's total assets of $5,000 to buy call options on stocks ($5,000 is the premium cost, not the underlying value of the calls). This portfolio is not leveraged in an accounting sense, because the total assets and net assets are equal at $5,000, with no liability or borrowing in the portfolio. However, the portfolio is clearly leveraged in an economic sense, because the returns will be proportionately much different from a portfolio that bought the stocks instead of the calls on the stocks.

Comment: Example 3 may or may not be considered leveraged. If considered leveraged, it could be argued that it is already on an all-cash basis, because there is no borrowing; the calls were purchased for cash. If there were to be any restatement, it would likely be to reflect the returns from a portfolio of the underlying stocks purchased for cash. Such a restatement would be forced to rely on hypothetical transactions involving the assumed prices at which the stocks could have been purchased, commissions, and so forth. The manager must disclose the strategy used, the risk/return profile of the strategy, and the impact on portfolio return.

Recommendation: Although this strategy might not be called leveraged, disclosure of the portfolio strategy employed is required. The principle that requires disclosure is in the spirit of the requirement pertaining to leverage—that the portfolio may experience unusual levels of risk or return due to the nature of the strategy employed. The returns need not be restated on an all-cash basis, because the portfolio is already truly all cash and any restatement to the comparable stock portfolio would rely on hypothetical transactions. Restatements that are not verifiable or do not rely upon actual transactions must be avoided.

Example 4: A manager holds $8,000 in stocks on margin and has sold $3,000 worth of stock index futures for an account with a net worth of $5,000. This portfolio is leveraged in an accounting sense in the same way as Example 1. It is not leveraged in an economic sense, because the futures hedge $3,000 of the stocks and the remaining $5,000 in stocks will then produce returns roughly equal to a portfolio that held $5,000 in the same stocks without borrowing.

Comment: Like Example 3, this example may or may not be considered leveraged. If leveraged, restatement to an all-cash basis could take two forms. First, the restatement could remove the gain or loss on the short futures (working from actual accounting records) and then proceed as in Example 1. The philosophy of this method is that the stocks, when viewed in the absence of the futures, are leveraged and must be restated accordingly. Second, the restatement could remove the gain or loss on the futures and adjust the stock portfolio (by using prices, commissions, etc.). Unlike the first method, this restatement goes to all cash by "unwinding" the margin transaction back to a $5,000 portfolio size. The philosophy of this method is that the sale of the futures was done as an alternative to actually selling $3,000 of stocks and, had the stocks been sold, there would have been no leverage. The manager must disclose the strategy used, the risk/return profile of the strategy, and the impact on portfolio return.

Recommendation: Disclosure of the portfolio strategy employed is recommended but not required. The portfolio, as given, is not leveraged relative to a fully invested, unleveraged stock portfolio and must not be expected to have unusual levels of risk or return. However, if the portfolio may employ actual leverage on occasion, or if the futures hedge is an active timing decision, then disclosure of the portfolio strategy employed would be required. In the former case, restatement to an all-cash basis is not needed. In the latter case, restatement may be recommended, depending on the actual strategy employed, the ability actually to execute the strategy on an all-cash basis, and the ability to restate based solely on actual transactions.

Example 5: A manager has sold short $1,000 in stocks and bought $1,000 in other stocks for an account with a net worth of $5,000. This portfolio is leveraged in an accounting sense, because selling short creates a liability to buy back the short stock and because total assets of $6,000 are greater than the net assets of $5,000. This portfolio is not leveraged in the strictest economic sense, because the portfolio may not produce a return much different from a portfolio of $5,000 in cash equivalents (assuming the long and short stocks are reasonably well correlated with each other and hedge each other).

Comment: Example 5 may not be leveraged according to the strict economic definition, but it is certainly leveraged on the basis of other investment considerations. The portfolio return clearly depends on the returns of the long versus short stocks. Moreover, the portfolio achieves this return without any outlay of cash (assuming the technical details of the use of proceeds from short sales is ignored). Because the portfolio could have been long and short $5,000 in stocks, just as easily as $1,000, it becomes clear that the return between the long and short stocks can be (or already is being) leveraged. Because it is unclear what all cash means with regard to short sales, this portfolio would not be restated to an all-cash position. The manager must disclose the strategy used, the risk/return profile of the strategy, and the impact on portfolio return.

Recommendation: Disclosure of the portfolio strategy employed is required because the portfolio may experience unusual levels of risk or return due to the nature of the strategy employed. The returns need not be restated to an all-cash basis, because the strategy cannot be executed without short sales, making all cash meaningless.

Example 6: Manager A has four clients for which securities are traded. Manager A prefers to have the clients trade on margin because of the greater leverage, but two clients do not permit trading on margin. Manager A has received $30,000 from each of the two clients who do not margin the securities and $15,000 from each of the two clients who do permit trading on margin. Manager A will trade all four accounts the same; that is, the same securities will be purchased or sold in the same quantities at the same time for each account. In month one, Manager A makes $50 in profit for each account.

Manager B is a futures trader and accepts an $800,000 account from a client who deposits $200,000 for margin. Manager B has one other client who also has allocated $800,000, and this client has all $800,000 deposited in the account. The trading for each account is identical. In month one, Manager B earns $5,000 in profit for each client.

Comment: This example illustrates a situation in which a manager trades some accounts within a composite at different levels of leverage. If the strategies for the portfolios are the same, they must be included in the same composite. To avoid performance distortion, the managers must restate the leveraged returns to an all-cash basis. Manager A must disclose the two accounts on margin and restate them to an all-cash basis as in Example 1. For Manager B, restatement requires that the returns must be calculated on the basis of the amount of assets allocated to the manager for investment (as opposed to only the amount deposited into the account for margin). Without restatement, composite results are distorted because of the "blended return" from portfolios trading at different levels of leverage.

At the end of the first month, Manager A and Manager B have earned the following returns on a leveraged basis:

$$\text{Manager A:} \quad \frac{\$200}{\$90,000} = 0.22\%$$

Manager B: $\dfrac{\$10{,}000}{\$1{,}000{,}000} = 1.00\%$

On an all-cash basis:

Manager A: $\dfrac{\$200}{\$120{,}000} = 0.17\%$

Manager B: $\dfrac{\$10{,}000}{\$1{,}600{,}000} = 0.63\%$

Recommendation: For Manager A, disclosure of the two accounts as leveraged is required, with whatever additional information about the use of leverage thoroughly discussed. The all-cash restatement must be computed and disclosed for the same reasons discussed in Example 1, as well as to avoid the reporting of "blended" returns. For Manager B, disclosure of the strategy employed is required, especially with respect to the client who has deposited only margin funds, because the portfolio may experience unusual levels of risk or return due to the strategy employed. Returns for this client need to be restated utilizing the amount of assets allocated to the manager, which must be disclosed. This allocation must be verifiable on the basis of the client agreement with the manager.

Derivatives: Example Scenarios

When presenting performance of derivative strategies for portfolios consisting primarily of other types of assets, the incremental return must be calculated by taking the difference between the total fund return and the return on the fund without the contribution of the derivative securities. The methodology used to do this must be disclosed and consistently applied, and it must be based on actual transactions and their accounting records.

The following three examples illustrate the issues in calculating performance for derivative strategies.

Example 7: This portfolio uses an option-overwriting strategy, whereby stocks are managed by one portfolio manager with the objective of producing competitive equity portfolio returns, while a second portfolio manager (within the same firm) writes covered call options on the stocks with the objective of adding incremental income to the portfolio. (This kind of overwriting strategy usually involves identification of stocks with little potential for much upside in the near term—but with good long-term potential—and normally uses out-of-the-money calls.)

Comment: In Example 7, the equity portfolio is managed to be a competitive equity portfolio in its own right. The overwriting of call options is clearly intended to produce incremental return. Up to here, the calculation and reporting of the return without the calls and the incremental return from the derivatives (i.e., calls) seems useful. But there is one major problem. When a call is exercised, the portfolio is obligated to deliver the stock or effectively sell the stock at the strike price of the call. The exercise of a call results in the portfolio selling a stock at a price at which it might not otherwise have been sold. For example, because a call gets exercised at a strike price of $35, the equity manager will be unable to sell at his intended price target of something higher, say $39. Thus, the return on the portfolio without the contribution of the calls does not actually measure what the equity manager would have done without the derivatives.

Recommendation: If included in an equity composite, disclosure of the portfolio strategy employed is required, because the covered call writing may have significant effects vis à vis an equity portfolio. The performance of the equity portfolio in the absence of the derivatives strategy cannot be accurately determined without the use of hypothetical transactions, as discussed previously. Thus, it is not recommended that the returns on the total fund without the derivatives or the incremental return be calculated.

Example 8: The portfolio uses a buy-and-write strategy, whereby stocks are purchased and covered call options are simultaneously written on the stocks. The manager's objective is to produce returns a few percentage points above cash-equivalent yields with low risk of negative returns. (This kind of buy-and-write strategy usually involves identifying stocks with little downside risk and normally uses in-the-money calls.)

Comment: Example 8 appears similar to Example 7, with both portfolios buying stocks and selling calls. In fact, it may be difficult to distinguish between the two by looking at a list of portfolio holdings. However, the role of the options in each case is different. In Example 8, the written call is intended to act more as a price hedge and, when coupled with the stock, to behave as a cash equivalent. In Example 7, on the other hand, the written call is explicitly intended not to be a price hedge but to produce incremental income. Likewise, the role of the stocks is different. In Example 7, the stocks are chosen on their merits as an equity investment. In Example 8, the stock and written call act as a hedged unit that cannot be considered separately in a meaningful way. A further complication of Example 8 is that trade orders for buy-and-writes may be placed on a net basis, such as "buy the stock and sell the call for a net debit of $17." This order may be filled either by buying the stock at $20 and selling the call at $3 or by buying the stock at $20.25 and selling the call at $3.25—either one netting a cost of $17. Either way, the effect on the total portfolio and its return is the same. But the calculation of returns without the contribution of derivatives would be affected, because it is important to the equity-only return if the stock cost was $20 or $20.25. Thus, for Example 8, the calculation and reporting of the return without the calls and the incremental return is not appropriate.

Recommendation: It is recommended that the portfolio not be included in an equity composite, because this particular portfolio has characteristics akin to cash management. If included in a cash management composite, disclosure of the portfolio strategy employed is required, because the returns will likely be significantly different from ordinary cash management returns. Because of the nature of the buy-and-write strategy, it is not meaningful, and hence not recommended, that the returns on the total fund without the derivatives or the incremental return be calculated.

Example 9: The portfolio is an enhanced index fund that uses derivatives to add incremental value above the S&P 500 stock index with little risk of underperforming. For example, the portfolio may sell a basket of S&P 500 stocks and replace them with U.S. Treasury bills (or other cash equivalents) and S&P 500 stock index futures.

Comment: A typical use of derivatives in Example 9 would involve selling stocks and simultaneously buying S&P 500 futures in an equal amount. Such trades are often done on the basis of the relative prices between the stocks and futures, i.e, when the futures are inexpensive relative to the stocks net of all transaction costs. The practical result of such a trade is that the stock portfolio absorbs some transaction cost (and a drag on the total stock performance), which is more than offset by incremental gains in the futures position. A further complication is that such trades are often done as principal trades where a net valuation spread between the stocks and futures is ensured, but the individual valuation of the stocks may be above or below the current quoted market. Again, this stock mispricing is more than offset in the futures pricing via the pricing of the net trade. Thus, the return on the portfolio without the contribution of the derivatives (i.e., the stock portfolio return) is actually influenced by the derivatives strategy, as in Example 8. While these effects on returns may be small, they are definitely significant. The stock portfolio is an index fund and a few basis points of "noise" in the return can represent significant and noticeable tracking error in a highly competitive index fund market.

Recommendation: If included in an equity composite, disclosure of the portfolio strategy employed is required, because the returns may be significantly affected by the derivatives. As discussed, it is not meaningful, and hence not recommended, that the returns on the total fund without the derivatives or the incremental return be calculated.

APPENDIX E
SEC POSITION ON ADVERTISING PERFORMANCE

Activities of investment advisors as defined in the Investment Advisers Act of 1940 are subject to the act and to the rules and regulations of the Securities and Exchange Commission. Whether or not investment advisors are registered with the SEC, their advertising of investment performance is subject to the SEC's scrutiny under Section 206 of the Investment Advisers Act—the general antifraud provisions—and Rule 206(4)-1. The term "advertising" is broadly defined in Rule 206(4)-1(b) as any written communication addressed to more than one person, or a communication in the media, relating, among other things, to securities investment services.

In a series of no-action letters beginning in 1986 with a letter involving Clover Capital Management, Inc. (publicly available October 28, 1986), the SEC staff has clarified its view of the requirements for investment advisor performance advertising. The requirements include disclosures in connection with the presentation of both actual and model results. Many of the disclosure requirements are contained in the Clover letter.

In a November 1989 letter (Securities Industry Association, publicly available November 27, 1989), the staff announced that for periods beginning May 27, 1990, all performance information must reflect deduction of an advisor's actual fees, but that for periods before that date, model fees that meet certain standards might be used.

In the second of two letters on the subject involving the Investment Company Institute (ICI, publicly available September 23, 1988), the SEC staff indicated that although performance information generally must be presented net of advisory fees, it is permissible in one-on-one presentations, as described in the letter, to present performance information without the deduction of advisory fees. The SEC staff defines one-on-one presentations as manager performance presentations to any client, prospective client, or affiliated group entrusted to consider manager selection and retention. Communications by managers can, therefore, be made to multiple representatives of a given prospect, even if there are several portfolios within the group. Any written performance presentation materials distributed to more than one client or prospect, in other than one-on-one presentations, must present performance results after deduction of management fees.

In presenting performance gross of fees, however, a number of additional disclosure requirements must be met. These were stated in the SEC staff letter, and are in addition to other disclosure requirements, as follows:

"We will not recommend any enforcement action to the commission if an investment adviser provides prospective clients performance results for advisory accounts on a gross basis in a one-on-one presentation as described in your letter. *This position is expressly conditioned upon the adviser providing at the same time to each client in writing* [emphasis added]:
1. "disclosure that the performance figures do not reflect the deduction of investment advisory fees;
2. "disclosure that the client's return will be reduced by the advisory fees and any other expenses it may incur in the management of its investment advisory account;
3. "disclosure that the investment advisory fees are described in Part II of the adviser's Form ADV; and
4. "a representative example (e.g., a table, chart, graph, or narrative) which shows the effect an investment advisory fee, compounded over a period of years, could have on the total value of a client's portfolio.

"We also would not recommend any enforcement action to the Commission if an investment adviser provides gross performance data to consultants as long as the adviser instructs the consultant to give the performance data to prospective clients of the adviser only on a one-on-one basis and the consultant provides the disclosure in (1) to (4) above.

"Finally, because this response is based upon your representations and is expressly conditioned upon an adviser or consultant providing the information set forth above, any different representations or conditions may require a different conclusion. Further, this response only expresses the Division's conclusions on the questions presented."

As quoted above, the SEC staff stated in the ICI letter that performance advertising that does not deduct advisory fees may be delivered to a consultant for the prospective client as long as the investment advisor restricts the consultant's use of the performance information to one-on-one presentation provided that the four disclosures specified above are made.

Managers should review the SEC pronouncements on performance presentation to determine their applicability and should be aware that certain additional disclosures in performance presentations are required by these pronouncements, especially in the Clover letter. Members should also consult their own legal or securities compliance advisors regarding applicable disclosure requirements.

APPENDIX F
PORTABILITY OF INVESTMENT RESULTS

The AIMR Performance Presentation Standards state that performance results of a past affiliation may not be used to represent the historical record of a new affiliation or a newly formed entity. The guiding principle, according to the standards, is that performance is the responsibility of the firm, not that of the individual portfolio manager. Changes in a firm's organization should not lead to alteration of composite results. Therefore, composites should include all accounts managed by a member of a firm, even if the individual responsible for the past results is no longer with the firm, and composites should not include portfolios managed by members of the firm before they joined the firm.

Performance data from a prior firm can, however, be used as supplemental information with the proper disclosures. The manager must give credit for the performance to the prior affiliation and describe his or her responsibilities at the previous employer. If the responsibilities are accurately portrayed, the market will determine how the record should be interpreted in light of the new affiliation or entity. The historical results of the previous affiliation cannot be linked with the results of the new affiliation or newly formed entity. The non-linking of records is a key factor.

In addition to the AIMR standards, a firm must also meet the SEC requirements of Section 206(4) regarding the use of past performance records. The following is an SEC staff-published summary of the no-action letter to Great Lakes Advisors, Inc., on the issue of portability.

> "The Division of Investment Management denied a request for no-action assurances from an investment adviser who wanted to use the performance data for the equity and fixed-income portions of its predecessor's investment portfolios. The successor firm began business on August 1, 1990, and wanted to use its predecessor's performance data from January 1, 1985, through July 1, 1990. During that period, the current manager for the equity portion selected equity securities by consensus among himself and two or three others, all of whom played significant roles in the decision-making process. The current manager for the fixed-income portion did not join the predecessor until November 1, 1988. The adviser argued that with appropriate disclosure, the use of the predecessor's performance data would not violate Rule 206(4) - 1(a)(5) under the Investment Adviser's Act, which

Association for Investment Management and Research

prohibits the use of false or misleading advertisements. With respect to the use of a predecessor's performance data, the staff has taken the position that it may not be misleading to do so if, among other things, no individual other than the successor's portfolio manager played a significant part in the performance of the predecessor's accounts, which the staff concluded was not the case in this instance."

In other words, the use of a predecessor's performance could be misleading if one or more individuals other than those at the successor organization played a role in the prior firm's strategy (other investment committee members), security selection (research analysts), or trading (if trading strategies are integral to the firm's overall strategy).

In addition, in a response of April 1992 to Great Lakes Advisers, Inc., the SEC also cited Fiduciary Management Associates, Inc. (publicly available February 2, 1984); Conway Asset Management, Inc. (January 27, 1989):

"We note that Rule 204-2(a)(16) under the Act generally requires an investment adviser to keep all documents that are necessary to form the basis for or demonstrate the calculation of the performance or rate of return of any or all managed accounts that the adviser uses in advertisements or other communications distributed to 10 or more persons. This requirement applies also to a successor's use of a predecessor's performance data."

According to the standards, if a newly formed entity constitutes a change in name or ownership only, i.e., all previous decision makers have transferred to the new entity, substantially all client assets have transferred, access to research records remains the same, and the management of the new firm is confident that there will be no misrepresentation in presenting the record of the previous firm as representing the historical record of the new entity, the guideline of "the record belongs to the firm" applies. This means that, in this instance, the record would stay with the firm that has simply undergone a change in name or ownership only.

APPENDIX G
SAMPLE PRESENTATIONS

Presentation 1. XYZ Investment Firm Performance Results January 1, 1984–December 31, 1993, Growth-Plus-Income Balanced Composite

Year	Total Return	Benchmark Return*	Number of Portfolios	Total Assets End of Period ($Millions)	Percent of Firm Assets
1984	12.1%	9.4%	6	$ 50	80%
1985	24.2	26.4	10	85	82
1986	17.0	16.4	15	120	78
1987	(3.3)	(1.7)	14	100	80
1988	15.8	12.8	18	124	75
1989	16.0	14.1	26	165	70
1990	2.2	1.8	32	235	68
1991	22.4	24.1	38	344	65
1992	7.1	6.0	45	445	64
1993	8.5	8.0	48	520	62

*Presentation of benchmark returns is not required.

Notes:
1. These results have been prepared and presented in compliance with the AIMR Performance Presentation Standards for the period 1/1/88 through 12/31/93. The full period is not in compliance. Prior to 1/1/88, not all fully discretionary portfolios were represented in appropriate composites. Composite results for the years 1984 through 1987 include the five largest institutional portfolios that were managed in accordance with the growth-plus-income strategy. These five accounts were consistently represented in the composite for the full period from 1984 through 1987.
2. Results for the full historical period are time weighted. From 1984 through 1990, results are calculated yearly, and the composites are asset weighted by beginning-of-year asset values. After January 1, 1991, composites are valued quarterly, and portfolio returns are weighted by using beginning-of-quarter market values plus weighted cash flows.
3. The benchmark: 60% S&P 500; 40% Lehman Intermediate Aggregate. Annualized Compound Composite Return = 11.9%. Annualized Compound Benchmark Return = 11.4%
4. Standard deviation in annual composite returns equals 8.24% versus a standard deviation in the yearly benchmark returns of 8.53%.
5. The dispersion of annual returns as measured by the range between the highest and lowest performing portfolios in the composite is as follows: 1984, 3.2%; 1985, 5.4%; 1986, 3.8%; 1987, 1.2%; 1988, 4.3%; 1989, 4.5%; 1990, 2.0%; 1991, 5.7%; 1992, 2.8%; 1993, 3.1%.
6. Performance results are presented before management and custodial fees. The management fee schedule is attached.
7. No alteration of composites as presented here has occurred because of changes in personnel or other reasons at any time.
8. Settlement-date accounting is used prior to 1990.
9. A complete list of firm composites and performance results is available upon request.

Association for Investment Management and Research

Presentation 2. XYZ Investment Firm Performance Results 1991 and 1992, Segment Returns for Medium-Risk Balanced Composite

Composite	Total Return	Equity-Only Return	Fixed-Income-Only Return	Cash-Only Return
1992 return	5.2%	5.0%	6.1%	3.3%
Percent of assets	100	45	45	10
1991 return	19.5	29.4	15.2	5.5
Percent of assets	100	44	36	20

Presentation 3. Sample Verification Statements

Level I: We have examined, according to the Level I requirements for verification, the accompanying Statement of Performance for XYZ Firm for the year ended December 31, 1993. In our opinion, the Statement of Performance presents fairly the composite performance of XYZ Firm for the year ended December 31, 1993, in conformity with the Performance Presentation Standards established by the Association for Investment Management and Research as set forth in the accompanying Notes.

Level II: We have examined, according to the Level II requirements for verification, the accompanying Statement of Performance for XYZ Firm for the year ended December 31, 1993. In our opinion, the Statement of Performance presents fairly the investment performance of XYZ Firm for the year ended December 31, 1993, in conformity with the Performance Presentation Standards established by the Association for Investment Management and Research as set forth in the accompanying Notes.

Accompanying Notes: The following information is extracted from and supplemented by the AIMR publication *Performance Presentation Standards*, 1993. This publication is the referral source of full discussion and elaboration of the summary points. Please see the enclosed Requirements, page ix; Mandatory Disclosures, page x; Recommended Guidelines and Disclosures, page xii; and Performance Presentation Standard IX, Verification, page 12.

Presentation 4. XYZ Realty Fund I Historical Performance, 1983–90

Year	Net Assets ($Millions)	Income (Loss)	Appreciation (Depreciation)	Total Gross Return
1983*	$175	7.0%	0.0%	7.0%
1984	194	9.0	4.0	13.3
1985	189	8.9	4.8	14.0
1986	194	8.4	2.8	11.4
1987	199	7.2	1.4	8.7
1988	195	7.4	−1.4	5.9
1989	203	6.5	0.8	7.3
1990	193	5.3	−9.0	−4.0

*Partial year, three quarters.

1. Returns do not include annual investment management fee of 1% of gross asset value.
2. Assets are appraised annually by an independent Member of the Appraisal Institute appraiser.
3. Income is based on accrual accounting and recognized at the commingled fund level.
4. Returns include interest income from short-term cash investments.
5. Returns are based on audited operating results.
6. Returns presented are net of leverage, which averaged 30% of asset value during 1990.
7. All properties of XYZ Realty Fund I have been included in performance presentation.
8. The sum of the income return component and appreciation return component may not equal the total gross return. This is due to the time-weighting of component quarterly returns.

APPENDIX H
AIMR STANDARD OF PROFESSIONAL CONDUCT III F

1. The financial analyst shall not make any statements, orally or in writing, which misrepresent the investment performance that the analyst or his firm has accomplished or can reasonably be expected to achieve.

2. If an analyst communicates directly or indirectly individual or firm performance information to a client or prospective client, or in a manner intended to be received by a client or prospective client ("Performance Information"), the analyst shall make every reasonable effort to ensure that such Performance Information is a fair, accurate, and complete presentation of such performance.

3. The financial analyst shall inform his employer about the existence and content of the Association for Investment Management and Research's Performance Presentation Standards and this Standard III F and shall encourage his employer to adopt and use the Performance Presentation Standards.

4. If Performance Information complies with the Performance Presentation Standards, the analyst shall be presumed to be in compliance with III F 2 above.

5. An analyst presenting Performance Information may use the following legend on the Performance Information presentation, but only if the analyst has made every reasonable effort to ensure that such presentation is in compliance with the Performance Presentation Standards in all material respects:

   "This report has been prepared and presented in compliance with the Performance Presentation Standards of the Association for Investment Management and Research."

Association for Investment Management and Research

INDEX

Accounting
    Accrual-basis 3, 11, 17, 26
    Cash-basis 3, 11, 17, 26
    Settlement-date 4, 9, 14, 44
    Trade-date 4, 9, 14, 44
Advertising performance 23, 61
AIMR Standards of Professional Conduct
    Compliance 2
    Section III E 3
    Section III F 3, 68
All-cash basis 17, 52–60
Asset-weighting (see also Size-weighting) 6, 11, 27, 28
Attribution 47

BAI method 20, 22, 23
Balanced portfolios (see also Multiple-asset portfolios/composites) . . 5, 8, 45
Benchmarks 11, 14, 15, 36, 45, 46

Carve-outs 14, 46, 47
Cash and cash equivalents 4, 8, 14, 17, 30–32
Cash flows 4, 19–22
Clover Capital Management, Inc. 61
Commingled funds 5
Composites
    Adding portfolios to 6
    Asset-weighting 6, 27, 28
    Balanced, segments of 5, 8
    Construction of 5–7
    Disclosures 8, 9
    Equal-weighting 6, 27, 28
    List of 7
    Model results 5
    Multiple assets 5, 8, 30
    Newly formed entity 7, 63, 64
    Number of 5
    Past affiliation 7, 63, 64
    Personnel changes 7, 63, 64
    Presentation of 7, 8

Association for Investment Management and Research

    Removing portfolios from 6
    Single assets 8, 9
    Switching between 6
    Taxable 5, 7, 8
    Tax-exempt 7, 8
Compliance
    International portfolios 2
    Retroactive 2, 10
    Taxable portfolios 2
    U.S. and Canadian portfolios 2, 3
Convertible securities 7
Currency
    Base 15, 44
    Hedging 15, 47
    Local 15, 44
    Overlay portfolios 15, 16

Daily valuation method 20
Derivatives 17, 52–60
Dietz method 20, 21, 23
Discretionary portfolios 5, 6
Dispersion (see also Risk and dispersion measures) 11, 12
Dividends 3

Equal-weighting 6, 27, 28
Exchange rate 14, 44
Ex-dividend date 3

Fee schedule 8, 23
Foreign taxes 14, 44

Great Lakes Advisors, Inc. 63
Gross-of-fees results 8, 23–25, 61

Hedging (see also Currency) 15, 46
Historical performance (see also Retroactive compliance) 2, 3, 9, 10
Hybrid instruments 7

Indexes 11, 12, 36, 44
Internal rate of return 22
International portfolios/composites (see also Compliance,
    Composites [Construction of] , Currency [Hedging,
    Overlay portfolios], and Performance calculations) . . 2, 13–16, 45–49

Association for Investment Management and Research

Investment Advisers Act of 1940 61
Investment Company Institute 61

Leverage 9, 17, 52–57
Linking of returns 3

Manager universes 36
Management fees 4, 8, 17, 23, 24, 61
Minimum-size portfolios 9
Model results 5
Multiple-asset portfolios/composites (see also Balanced portfolios)
    Cash allocation in 8–11, 30–32
    Presentation of 9, 10
    Rebalancing frequency 12
    Segment returns 8, 9, 11

Net-of-fees results 4, 8, 9, 23–26, 61
Newly formed entity 7
Non-fee-paying portfolios 5, 9
Normal portfolios 37

One-on-one presentation 61

Performance calculations
    Accrual accounting 3, 11, 17, 26
    Cash, cash equivalents, or substitute assets 4, 17
    Cash-basis accounting 3, 11, 17, 26
    Commencement dates 4
    Fees 4, 23
    Linking 3, 29
    Time-weighted rate of return 3, 19, 20
    Total return 3, 19
    Valuation periods 3, 4, 10, 16, 29
Portability 63–64
Portfolios
    Actual 5
    Balanced 5
    Commingled 5
    Currency overlay 15, 16, 48, 49
    Discretionary 5, 6
    Fee-paying 5
    Multiple-asset 5, 9, 12

    Nondiscretionary 5, 6
    Non-fee-paying 5
    Normal 11, 37
    Performance calculations 3–5
    Size limits 6
    Single-asset 5, 9
    Taxable 2
Pricing 4

Rate of return
    Daily valuation method 20, 21
    Internal 22
    Modified BAI method 20, 22
    Modified Dietz method 20, 21
    Time-weighted 3, 19, 20
Real estate 16, 17
Reporting periods 7
Restrictions 5, 6
Retroactive compliance 2, 3, 7, 9–11, 32
Revaluation 4
Risk and dispersion measures
    Benchmarks 11
    Beta 11, 34
    Calculation of 33–43
    External 8, 11, 33
    Indexes 11, 12, 36
    Internal 8, 12, 37
    Presentation of 11, 12, 42
    Quartile dollar dispersion 41
    Range 12, 41
    Sharpe measure 35
    Standard deviation 11, 12, 33, 38
    Treynor measure 35

Securities and Exchange Commission 4, 23, 61–64
Settlement date 4, 9, 14
Short-selling 17
Single-asset portfolios/composites 8, 10, 11
Size-weighting (see also Asset-weighting) 6, 11, 27, 28
Standard deviation 11, 12, 33, 38
Supplemental information 8, 9

Tax rate 5, 14
Taxable portfolios/composites 2, 5, 6
Tax-exempt securities 7
Time-weighted rate of return 3, 19, 20
Total return 3, 19
Trade date 4, 9, 14
Treynor measure 35

Unit trusts 5

Valuation period 3, 4, 10, 16, 29
Verification
    Attest 12
    Level I 12, 13
    Level II 12, 13

Withholding taxes 14, 44
Wrap fees 4

Association for Investment Management and Research